Saving
Russia
and raising four kids

Schizophrenia and
Solo Parenthood

ECHO BOOKS

Bob Breen

First published in Sydney by Fast Books in 1995 by Wild and Woolley Pty Ltd, 16 Darghan Street, Glebe, NSW 2037 for Mavor Pty Ltd.

Second Edition published for Mavor Pty Ltd in Canberra in 2017 by Barrallier Books Pty Ltd, trading as Echo Books, Registered Office: 35-37 Gordon Avenue, West Geelong, Victoria 3220, Australia.

www.echobooks.com.au

2ND EDITION

National Library of Australia Cataloguing-in-Publication entry.

Creator: Breen, Bob, 1952- author.

Title: Saving Russia and raising four kids : schizophrenia and solo

parenthood / Bob Breen.

Edition: 2nd edition.

ISBN: 9780648110705 (paperback)

Subjects: Breen, Gwen, 1925-. Schizophrenics--Biography. Women--Mental health.

Women volunteers in social service--Biography. Single mothers--Biography.

Book layout and design by Peter Gamble, Canberra.
Set in Garamond Premier Pro Display, 12/17 and Minerva Small Caps.

www.echobooks.com.au

Contents

A Tribute

A tribute to those people who supported and prayed for me during my journey of healings to mental stability

Gwen Breen

circa 1995

I thank my parents for their practical support in taking me and my four children into their home after my first episode of mental illness and trip to Royal Park in 1960.

My sisters and brothers for their support

My very special thanks go to my children who have loved me through the difficult times, especially for being patient with me when I was trying to cease my prescribed drugs. I tried nine times and failed nine times. Helen said she had tried being kind and [then] she got angry with me. It [her anger] paid off as I vowed to continue with *Melleril* that has been taken off the market as it has been found to affect the heart and liver.

I am now on *Szypresca* and it keeps me well. I wish also to ask my children to forgive me for putting them through the traumas caused by my trying to beat my schizophrenia. Helen had to get angry with me before I discovered I was trying to beat a chemical imbalance in my brain and I cannot do anything about that, no matter how hard I try. So, I am on *Szypresca* for the rest of my life. It has not been easy for them, but they came through with flying colours.

Thanks also to my children's spouses [Diane, Rhonda, Don and Harry] whom I call my adopted children, they welcome me to their homes bi-annually.

I would like to thank the following priests for their assistance. I found them more helpful than the doctors I attended in my quest for healings.

Father Max [Barrett], Editor of the [Redemptorist Order] *Majellan* Magazine who helped me realize I had been feeling guilty about my sexual molestation at seven years of age. I started to tell him my story about the molestation and, before I completed the first sentence, he said two wonderful and healing words without hesitation, 'Not guilty'. A couple of days later I found myself hanging on the towel rail in my kitchen with my body helplessly wracked with deep sobbing and saying to myself, 'And it wasn't even my fault.' I consider that this experience was my first healing.

I love him dearly for his contribution to [improving] my mental health and well-being, and his continuing friendship and support. Father Max was crucial to my journey to wellness. He kept in touch with me through wonderful caring letters and, most importantly, after I knew the importance of forgiveness in getting well, he said I did not need to feel warmly towards them [those whom I had forgiven].

Father Gerard [Dowling], a talk-back host on radio in Melbourne, for making me feel special. He wrote an article in *The Advocate* [Catholic newspaper in Melbourne] for 'deserted wives' pointing out that we have to cope with shock, hurt and grieving—I put a 'big tick' to 'shock' and 'hurt'—but grieving—I was not doing that [I said to myself]. It took me 18 months after reading that article to realise that [grieving] was just what I was doing.

One day I knocked off work at the Bayside Area Scout Shop at 5 to go and pick up Melissa [grand daughter] in St Kilda. Going into the traffic on Nepean Highway at that time of night was no fun. I got stuck in the traffic and then it hit me. I was grieving and there was a persistent feeling of self-pity there as well. Both feelings horrified me and I was able to give them away which was a great relief and another healing. Once I realised that I was grieving, I was able to cope with that depressing and sometimes angry feeling—another healing. I had been grieving for 20 years.

Father Gerard was giving us a retreat at Pallotti College in Warburton in Victoria for solo parents. He wasn't even facing us as he went to a suitcase to get out a book. He said, 'Of course you can't forget.' I thought to myself, 'You bloody fool, Gwen, that's just what you have been trying to do. Trust you to be trying to do the impossible. So I gave that [trying to forget] away.

Father Bill who made me feel I was a loving person, who also deserved to be loved.

Marie [Spittall] who was my back-stop for all those years when I was coordinating retreats at Majellan House and was so terribly unsure of myself—her affirmation got me through. She is a very dear friend.

Father Laurie for listening to me rave on without interrupting for at least a half an hour about my disappointment with Father Maurice who made me feel guilty about the breakdown of my marriage. The Holy Spirit worked beautifully through him to our mutual benefit.

Lance at the Hofbauer Centre for making me realise that life would continue to have its ups and downs and that I would have to ride with the punches.

The four people who tried to help me cope with the complete devastation the priest [Father Maurice] had caused me when I went to him a few days after Keith had told me he'd committed adultery with Jan and had a baby. I did not really need another 'kick in the guts' after blacking out when Keith told me his news. None of those four people told me to forgive that priest. The Holy Spirit Himself had to do that. I was angry with that priest from 1959 to 1994. I thank the Holy Spirit for that healing.

Margaret from Open House for teaching us that we did not have to examine our consciences on our feelings because feelings are neither 'right' nor 'wrong'. It's what you do with the feelings that counts.

Sister Damian for her compassion.

Father Victor and Father Pat [from Majellan House] for praying over me.

My cousin, Kaye, for understanding.

Leslie and Cynthia who taught me heaps and helped me through the healing process of my grandmother's suicide.

Peg [Fitzgerald], my best friend—ever ready to listen—she opened a new world to me—introducing me to Pax Christi, World Conference for Peace and the World Council of Churches.

Dorothy [Whitten], [wife of Jim, Commissioner for the Bayside Area Scouts] for telling me she trusted me when I was working closely with her husband. It was like a breath of fresh air gently blowing over me.

Norma and Vic for being there when Cassie, my granddaughter died in a cot death and for their continuing prayful support and friendship.

Anne [younger sister] who tells me that I'm 'lovely' and always had a listening ear.

The 70 people who responded to Helen's request for letters telling me how I'd touched their lives. They made me feel very warm and affirmed. I received those letters on my 70th birthday—a real warm fuzzy [feeling].

Father Frank and Father Reg, who taught us such a lot on the Redemptorist Lay Community Courses they organised for solo parents. One of the courses was specifically to teach us to minister to solo parents.

Ex-Wrans Association for being there when I decided after my bad experiences with men, that I would keep socialising at all-women functions.

Reverend Frank Hartley for allowing me to be part of the Supporting Mothers' Association.

The Women's Action Alliance for teaching me a great deal—Nance and Aileen for being my sounding boards.

Universities of the Third Age—I find this one of the most exciting experiences I have been involved in.

Catholic solo parents for their warmth and loving.

Graham for telling me that it was my thinking making me ill. I realised that I had to have complete 'Confidence in God, myself, my children and my fellow man'. I had to overcome my feeling of apprehension—another healing.

Elizabeth and her Marian Group. She just smiles when I say, 'I've come for my Sassafras 'fix'.' I come away from this group feeling spiritually and physically refreshed.

Bern [Melican], my nephew, who at my 70th birthday party told me he loved me.

Rolinda in the Philippines for her continuing prayful support. Her hospitality in Manila was 'something to behold'. It was 'out of this world'. I cannot thank her enough.

Margaret, my Canadian friend, for her help towards my philanthropic work, especially in connection with the Philippines.

Seraphima, my Russian friend in Moscow, who by her example in tending to grandchildren and grandmothers has made me realise that my love for the Russian people was not misplaced.

Helen, Don, Phil, Faye and the Lions Club for their help with my 'Clothes for Russia' project.

Evanne for her co-ordination of the luncheons stemming out of the Majellan Retreats for deserted wives.

Jean [Pink], ever ready for practical advice, love and affirmation.

Pat for her prayful support.

Trish for her kindness.

Marie and Edna for their friendship and love.

Maureen, ever ready for her good laugh.

Special thanks to my overseas friends for keeping in touch.

Thanking people who have touched your life always leaves one open to forget someone—so I include all my friends for their friendship.

I consider myself healed now, but I cannot say that I'm cured of my schizophrenia, but the healings certainly make life bearable. I am most grateful to those priests who helped me.

Preface

I wrote *Gwen Saves Russia* in 1995 to commemorate Gwen Breen's first 70 years of life. She was retired and enjoying reasonably good health. Her four children were married, employed, owned homes and had healthy offspring. Her older daughter, Helen, thoughtfully rang over 80 numbers she sleuthed out of Gwen's well-thumbed notebook of contacts and received over forty letters and notes from family and friends who congratulated Gwen on her 70th birthday and wrote about her impact on their lives. These letters, as well as my gratitude for Mum's fortitude and unconditional love, prompted me to write a short biography in order to affirm her, and educate and inspire others, as well as to leave a family history for following generations.

This edition completes the story. By the time she died suddenly—alone and in care—in Blackburn, Melbourne on 17 January 2012 aged 87 she had been through several health crises and some of the vicissitudes of life had impacted her four children since her 70th Birthday. Inter-generational effects of paternal abandonment and consequent troubled childhoods caught up with them. Each in their own way found strength in Gwen's stoic example as she battled mental and physical illnesses for another 17 years, telling everyone who asked, 'These are the happiest days of my life.'

Between 1995 and 2012 Mum shared new perspectives on her life with me and sent more family information. Importantly, she offered further insights and more of her wisdom. At her funeral I said that she had not been a great Australian in the usual sense of how society understands and measures greatness, but that Gwen had been a great mother and friend who touched many people's lives in positive ways. Father Gerard Dowling, a former Melbourne Roman Catholic talkback radio priest, who co-celebrated Gwen's requiem Mass, disagreed with me saying during his closing remarks, 'I disagree with her son about Gwen not being a great Australian. Gwen Breen was a great Australian by all measures of what it is to be 'great.' This book, mindful of the temptation of hagiography, explores Gerard Dowling's assessment.

I would like to thank my Auntie Barbara for the information for the Prologue, Origins of an Australian Family and my brother Peter for collecting the photographs that illustrate Gwen Breen's journey. I acknowledge and thank my Duntroon classmate and good mate, Ian Gordon, founder of Echo Books, for his advice, encouragement and professionalism, Peter Gamble for his design and typesetting and Jenny Warren for the Index

The book is for my siblings, my family and Gwen Breen's O'Meara-Allsop clan. My hope is that my brother and sisters and my children, as well as other members of the clan, find this account of Gwen's life useful in their lives and those of their children, as well as their children's children. It is important to know where you have come from and to draw both inspiration—as well as warning—from the lives of ancestors.

Bob Breen
Canberra 2016

Prologue–Origins of an Australian Family

Gwen Breen had Irish Catholic and British Protestant blood in her veins. Contemporary Irish roots relevant to the origins of Gwen's family in Australia began with Patrick O'Meara, a Roman Catholic, who was born in Aughrim, County Wicklow, Ireland, on 5 April 1833 to father, Michael O'Meara, and mother, Terranora Silk. Patrick married Jane Jameson, a former Protestant who had converted to Catholicism, on 18 June 1857 at St Michael's Church, Ballinasloe. Deemed to be a 'mixed marriage', the ceremony and Mass were conducted secretly with only close family in attendance. Jane's parents were Andrew Jameson and Phoebe Dolphin. [1]

Suggesting a whirlwind romance, Jane had already made arrangements to immigrate to South Australia with her brother, Creighton (15 years old) and sister, Rebecca (9 years old), when she married Patrick. She and her two siblings arrived in Adelaide on the ship *Lady Ann* in November 1857. Patrick joined Jane and her siblings later. Their first child, Rebecca, was born on 19 October 1860. They would go on to have eight more children, some of whom would die in infancy: (Patrick Jr) (1862), Michael (1865), Phoebe (1867), Margaret (1869), Mary Jane (1872), Jane (1874), Thomas (1876) and Kit (1878). Patrick died at 48 years of age on 12 September 1881 three years after his ninth child, Kit, was born. Jane passed on 25 June 1924 in her late 80s, both were buried next to each other at Eastern Cemetery, Geelong. There does not appear to be an account of how Jane fared as an immigrant Irish widow with six surviving children aged from 21 to five years old in 1881.

Patrick and Jane's oldest son, Patrick, who was born in 1862 and called by his second name John, was to become Gwen's paternal grandfather.[2] Grandfather John, normally called Jack, married, Mary Jane Hanson and she gave birth to Gwen's father Robert, who was known as Bob, on 6 March 1906 after several miscarriages. Bob had an adopted older sister, Jessie, a younger brother, Andrew and a half-sister, Ettie.

Gwen's British family tree on her maternal side becomes relevant to Australia with the marriage of John Allsop and Ellen Fearn, both from Tissington, Derbyshire, on 27 March 1843. They emigrated from Plymouth, England, accompanied by two daughters, Sarah and Elizabeth, on 12 March 1852, arriving at Hobson's Bay Wharf, Williamstown, near Melbourne on board the ship *Chongrinhee* on 5 July 1852 with a new baby, Samuel, who had been born on 1 June 1852 during the voyage.

Samuel Allsop, the 'high seas' baby born on the *Chongrinhee,* married Eliza Foster, who was Australian-born from Balaclava, at St George's Church, Malvern, Melbourne, on 26 April 1876. Samuel would die at Alfred Hospital, Melbourne on 20 February 1911 three years after Eliza who passed on 5 March 1908. They left four boys and a daughter: William, called Bill, Samuel, called Sam, Robert (1880), called Bob, Charles, called Charlie, and Violet. Bill, Sam, Bob and Charlie would go on to serve in the First World War with the 1st Australian Imperial Force (1st AIF).

William John Allsop, who was called Bill, Samuel and Eliza's oldest son, married May Blanche Kyme, and became Gwen's maternal grandparents after giving birth to Nellie May Allsop, Gwen's mother, on 11 January 1904.

*Patrick John O'Meara, known as John/
Jack, as a young man.*

*Mary Jane Hanson, known as Jane, as
a young woman.*

*Mary Jane (Jane) O'Meara with her sons
Andrew Jameson (Andy) and Robert
Jameson (Bob)*

*Andy O'Meara dressed to serve
Australia in WW1*

William John (Bill) Allsop railway ganger and punter

May Blanch Kyme in her early years

Granny May Allsop (left rear) with her daughter Nellie and Nellie's first three children Gwen, Barbara and Brian O'Meara

Nell O'Meara's sister Valerie (Val) Allsop in her early years

Bill and May would go on to have another daughter Valerie, called Val, in 1906 and a 'surprise' baby boy, William, called Billy, in 1914. Bill's brother, Sam, married May's sister, Annie. Another brother, Bob, married Gladys and Charlie, who would go on to lead a life of crime, remained single.

Early Years 1925-1948

On 11 January 1925 Gweneth Patricia O'Meara was born in a private hospital at Balaclava, Melbourne, on her mother, Nellie's, 21st birthday. She was given the first name of the doctor who delivered her, Dr Gweneth Wisewould.

*A long term family friend Dr Gweneth
Wisewould (right) with Nell later in life*

A few weeks later, Gwen was baptised at Holy Angels Church, Balaclava on 1 February by Reverend Michael O'Sullivan and consecrated to the Blessed Virgin Mary. Her godparents were her father's brother, Andrew O'Meara and his aunt, Jane Shaw. In that same year, builders completed St Finbar's School Hall, East Brighton, and adorned it with the inscription 'AMDG 1925'. ('AMDG' was a Latin acronym for 'All for the Honour and Glory of God'.) Gwen's younger brother, Brian, used to joke years later that the inscription must have been put there by his parents, and was really Latin for 'A Magnificent Daughter, Gwen'.[3]

Robert Jameson (Bob) O'Meara in his prime

Toddler Gwen with her parents Nell and Bob

Gwen's father, Robert (Bob) Jamieson O'Meara, was a bus driver who would later become a commercial traveller for Dunlop tyres. Her mother, Nellie May (nee Allsop), worked as a cashier in a butcher's shop. Bob was a tall, lantern-jawed man who came from a working class Irish Catholic family (see Chapter 1). He had not completed his secondary education because he had been expelled from De La Salle College, Malvern, for knocking out a Lasallian brother in retaliation for the brother hitting him on the head with a book.

Bob O'Meara with his first son and third child Brian circa 1931

Grandfather Jack saw his son Bob dressed for service in WW2

Bob's father was Patrick John 'Jack' O'Meara, a wiry railway ganger and shop steward with the Railway Workers' Union, who lived near the railway line in Toorak. Jack was a stylishly-dressed man with a shock of white hair, who was always well-groomed and tidy.

He eschewed any discussion of religion or politics. He walked with his hands behind his back in the same manner as when inspecting railway sleepers. One of his favourite sayings was, 'It's a bugger being poor, but there's no need to look it.' Jack was tough and fit. He took a cold shower every day of his life, and according to Gwen, he could still run hard for a tram at 82 years of age.

Jack was a generous man with a ribald sense of humour. He spoiled Gwen, his first grandchild, with boiled lollies and plenty of affection and attention. Once, after reading in a newspaper article that kissing was unhygienic, he hooted, 'But what a way to go!' He also quipped regularly to his wife, Mary, 'I do not know about love, Mary, but let's start with me feeling your bum.' The problem with Jack was his punting. Gwen remembered: 'He gambled away the roof over my grandmother's head. [Eventually] they lived separately on the same property. Grandfather was in a tent in the backyard and Granny Mary lived in the rented house.'

Mary (nee Hanson), Jack's wife, was a gracious, loving and wise country woman who battled to make ends meet under the financial pressure of Jack's gambling. Gwen remembers that Mary was respected wherever she went. Gwen used to visit Granny Mary at her home in Osment Street, Toorak. The house had a well-established garden with all sorts of flowers. Gwen recalled:

> I remember her saying, 'How can anyone not believe in God when you see this.' It was a snowdrop. It had a fluted edge trimmed in green, with a dot of green on each flute. I've never forgotten that. Every time I see a snow drop, I think of her.

Mary was a compassionate and loving role model for Gwen. During the Depression years she helped many families by donating home-made jams and preserves to those in need.

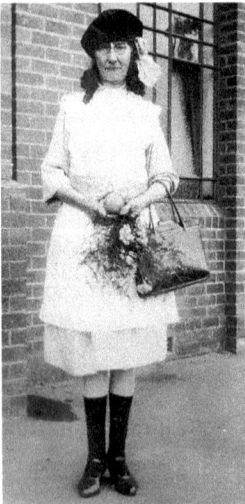

Jane O'Meara in younger times

Gwen recalls that some of Jack's siblings were strong personalities. Aunties Jane, Rebecca and Kit were Jack's sisters. Jane was the most domineering personality who, in Gwen's opinion, sought inappropriate influence in Jack's marriage. She visited every Sunday to attend the O'Meara family's traditional roast lunches and wanted to know everything about family business. She a close interest in the progress of Gwen, her godchild.

Nellie May Allsop, Gwen's mother, was from a lower middle class Protestant family of British immigrants with interesting politics and a couple of 'black sheep'. Nell's father, Bill Allsop, ran a hay and corn store in Collingwood, Melbourne, for several

Bob O'Meara with his in-laws Bill and May Allsop

years before losing most of his hearing and having to work as a gardener to make ends meet. He was a local political identity serving as the Secretary of the St Kilda Branch of the Australian Labor Party for many years. One of his memorable sayings was, 'We fought for the Arbitration Court and now the silly buggers (the workers) are not taking any notice of it.'

Bill's wife, May (nee Kyme), was a socialist and politically active in the Peace Movement that developed a strong voice in Australian politics by the end of the First World War and into the 1920s and 30s. During the war she had supported Melbourne's Archbishop Mannix's campaign against conscription. Gwen remembers hearing Granny May having long conversations about how the world would be a more peaceful and better place if socialists were in charge. May's socialism was more utopian and utilitarian than the ideology of the emerging Australian Communist party that falsely portrayed itself as a party for peace rather than world domination. May put her social conscience into practice by helping others in need. A regular visitor to the local Court House, she assisted young women in trouble with the law by putting them in contact with charitable organisations that could provide material support and some religious guidance. Like Granny Mary, Granny May too was a compassionate and loving role model for Gwen.

Grandfather Bill and Granny May kept high social standards. Granny May had gone into service in the wealthy households of Toorak at the tender age of ten years. She worked as a maid until she married Bill. Bill and May insisted on meticulous ritual for meals, and proper dress and deportment that emulated the wealthy classes. Gwen remembers:

> She was a lovely looking woman with never a hair out of place. Her home was sterile clean; you could eat off the floor. She (had) worked for people in Toorak—a doctor I think. Consequently her home was always conducted in a manner befitting the gentry. She had all Willow-patterned crockery and her table linen and cutlery were of the finest. She was an excellent cook. Her meals were served beautifully.

Bill Allsop and his brother Sam, who lost a leg during the Gallipoli Campaign were pillars of society compared to their brothers, Charlie and Robert, called Bob, who were both known to the Victorian police after serving with the Australian Imperial Force in the First World War. Charlie was the more notable due to his membership of Melbourne's most notorious gang led by well-publicised criminal Squizzy Taylor.[4] Charlie was a stand-over man who also fenced stolen goods and was charged but acquitted of armed robbery. Gwen had a vivid memory of Uncle Charlie trying to sell 'hot' radios to her father at a relative's funeral. Charlie Allsop appeared in court many times for a variety of offences but did not appear to have been jailed. His '15 minutes of fame' was escorting Squizzy Taylor's widow to Taylor's funeral on 30 October 1927 after Taylor was killed in 'a revolver duel' with John 'Snowy' Cutmore in Carlton on 27 October.[5]

Another of Nell's uncles, Robert Allsop, who like his brothers Charlie, Sam and Bill had joined the 1st Australian Imperial Force (46th Battalion, 2nd Pioneer Battalion and 55th Battalion respectively) to fight in the First World War, was an SP bookmaker.[6] Indeed, he was a one-armed bookmaker having lost an arm in France on 5 April 1918. This occupation involved quoting starting prices, hence 'SP', before a race and taking bets by telephone or at places away from the race track, an illegal activity because betting was only authorised at the race track. This type of bookmaking was very popular with Australian punters because it was convenient. SP bookmaking came into disrepute after some instances of corruption, malpractices and strongarm tactics directed at getting losing punters to pay their debts.[7]

Bob O'Meara, Gwen's father, training a cyclist,
possibly Bill Spencer

Gwen was an only child for three and half years until her sister, Barbara, arrived in 1928. She was referred to as 'First Born' and 'grew up in a loving atmosphere.'[8] Her brother Brian was born on 17 September 1931, and like Barbara, would go on to attend St Finbar's School. Brian would go on to win a diocesan scholarship to St Leo's School, Malvern, and later a scholarship to De La Salle College, Malvern, his father's and uncles' alma mater.

Gwen's earliest memories included time spent living in Paddington in Sydney where Bob drove double-decker buses for 12 months. When the family returned to Melbourne Bob and Nell rented a home in Empress Street, East St Kilda. Bob was a talented cyclist who turned down an offer from a famous cyclist of the day, Bill Spencer, to go to the USA to compete for money.

Dr Wisewould intervened to advise Bob that Nell was receiving treatment for a sensitive medical condition and that toddler, Gwen, and her baby sister, Barbara, who had been born on 20 July 1928, and baptised at Our Lady of Lourdes church, Armadale, by Reverend Father M.I. O'Brien on 12 August, were too young to travel that far.[9]

Bob had a sense of duty and responsibility to his wife and daughter, Gwen, and baby, Barbara. He saved his money and in late 1928, when Gwen was three years old, moved his family into what was known as a 'Bank' house in Ward Street in the emerging middle-class suburb of East Brighton. He had been allocated the land at an auction for 10 pounds and the house was built for 900 pounds. There were no sealed roads and plenty of land around to keep two cows and a horse, Darkie, who had been a race horse in its day, as well as another horse with a lesser pedigree.

Gwen attended St Finbar's Catholic Primary School, East Brighton, which was 'over the back' from Ward Street, as would all of her siblings after her. Peg Fitzgerald, a fellow student, remembers Gwen as a neatly dressed girl who achieved excellent results in her studies, and who was popular and active in sports and playground games. Gwen loved horse riding and basketball. Her brother, Brian wrote later:

> I can recall Gwen being an avid horse rider and she was often seen galloping across the paddocks of East Brighton on the back of one of Mrs Dennis' 'hacks for hire'. Her other love was the basketball court where her diminutive frame was often pitted against very tall, physically superior girls from neighbouring Catholic schools. (Because of) her father's coaching, Gwen was never over-awed by the physical dominance of her opponents. She showed a spirit that would have labelled her 'a little Aussie battler' as she took on the might of the area's 'giants'.[10]

Ward Street, East Brighton was a lively, vibrant place and full of children playing cricket, football and net ball. During the summers, fathers sat in groups on porches drinking beer and smoking. One of Gwen's happy memories is of her father, Bob, making ice-cream. The O'Meara and the McGinley children, who had lost their father in an industrial accident, would gather around Bob, watching and waiting, eager to taste the new batch. The O'Meara family had two cows and a 'Cherry Churn', so there was always plenty of milk, cream and butter.

After Barbara came Anne Theresa who was born on 7 January 1930 and baptised on 26 February by Father P. Ryan at St Joan of Arc, Brighton.[11] Brian arrived in the following year on 17 September 1931 and was baptised on 18 October by Father P. Ryan at St Joan of Arc's Church, Brighton.[12] Bob and Nell's fifth and last child, Peter William was born on 4 February 1933 and baptised on 21 March 1933 by Father P. Ryan at St Joan of Arc's Church, Brighton.[13]

Three primary school age sisters, Anne, Barbara and Gwen at Ward Street

Though the Depression cast a pall over the well-being of many Australians, the 1930s were happy years for Gwen and her brothers and sisters. Bob was a caring and active father, and a keen sportsman in rowing and cycling. While he rowed for the Albert Park Rowing Club, Gwen and her siblings would catch yabbies in Albert Park Lake. The children went to cycling meetings with Bob and watched him compete against future international sports representatives, such as Hubert Opperman.

Bob O'Meara had risen above his own family circumstances to become a responsible husband and father. He was ashamed of his father's gambling and had no time for betting on horse races. He had saved his money to buy the house at Ward Street and provided for his large family during the Depression years. Like his mother, he was conscious of the plight of others, frequently donating his time and money to those in need. He would often say, 'But for the grace of God, there go I.'

Bob consideration extended to Nell, who managed poor health for most of her life. He bought her the first washing machine in Brighton so that she would not have to wash the clothes and linen of their growing family in a large copper. He also employed maids to assist Nell to maintain the household. Gwen remembers Rita, a young Indigenous woman being with the family for some time:

> She was a marvellous needle woman and could sketch very well. She used to tell us stories of the bush. Unfortunately, Rita was taken in by what I guess was a pimp and she turned to

prostitution [at Fitzroy]. My father tried to get her back four
times. After she returned [to Fitzroy] each time, he gave up and
left her with the white man.[14]

For school holiday treats, the O'Meara kids travelled north of
Melbourne to Maldon to stay with their Auntie Ettie and Uncle Jack. Ettie
was Granny May's step sister. May and Ettie's mother had three husbands
and several children by each of them, so there was a blended family of half-
sisters and brothers with different surnames. Ettie and Jack were warm
generous people who loved Gwen and her younger brothers and sisters.
Their daughter, Pat, was like a big sister to Gwen and her son, Johnnie, like
a brother. Ettie, Jack, Pat and Johnnie were Gwen's favourite relatives on
Nell's side of the family, after Nell's mother, Granny May. She recalls:

> Auntie Ettie had a dress up box in the cow shed and we were
> allowed to use the clothing, shoes and hats to play dress ups. She
> made her own soap, bread and butter. She made puftaloons out
> of the dough left over from the bread. They were delicious—a
> sort of doughnut. But nothing compares to the taste these days.
> ... Uncle Jack had his own bees. The fresh bread and homemade
> butter topped with honey from Uncle Jack's bees was something
> else. A real treat. And of course the bread was quivering fresh.
> I feel that Auntie Ettie was a truly Christian woman, taking
> five children and a Mum (Nell) into her home. I will always
> have happy memories of the walks she used to take us on, her
> laughter and her love.[15]

One of Ettie and Jack's daughters, Kaye would become one of Gwen's
closest friends over the coming years. Kaye was a loyal friend who eschewed
marriage to care for her severely-disabled sister, Carole.

Not all of Nell's relatives were so kind to Gwen. An incident occurred
in 1932 when Gwen was seven years old that was to remain a repressed,
destructive and malignant secret for many years. While her parents were
away one afternoon a teenage male relative sexually molested her in the
hallway of her home at Ward Street. He threatened dire consequences if she
told anyone about his efforts to gratify himself. Gwen loved this young man

Barbara and Gwen play dress-up

The four kids are joined by the last child Peter

with the innocence of a child. The only reason she suspected that his actions were immoral was when he warned her not to tell the priest about what had happened in Confession, a Catholic sacrament she had been recently introduced to in preparation for her First Communion, another Roman Catholic sacrament.

This betrayal and theft of childhood innocence physically and mentally hurt Gwen, and forever lodged deeply into her mind. The memory and life-long impact of this event proved to be permanent. Gwen kept the secret and continued friendly contact with the relative, but never again trusted to be alone with him. Indeed, she would write to him during her teenage years. In her adult years Gwen would become confused about 'good' and 'bad' touching between men and women, and what men expected of women sexually. Sex was never discussed in the O'Meara family. Nell, conditioned by her own upbringing and culture, never took Gwen aside to explain anything about 'the birds and the bees'.

In 1936 when Gwen was 11 years of age a failed family business venture interrupted the halcyon days at Ward Street. Bob and Nell had opened a guesthouse in Healsville, despite having five active young children to manage. Healsville turned out for Gwen to be a cold and unhappy place. A polio epidemic Australia hit around this time and Victorians were discouraged from travelling because of the risks of infection. All of the guesthouses in Healsville had unexpected vacancies for months. Bob and Nell were forced to sell up, and return to Ward Street in financial straits. Bob worked for 12 months for a neighbour Mr Pimm who had an 'ice round'. [16] Before securing a job as a Commercial Traveller with Dunlop tyres.

Gwen's sexual molestation would trouble her for the rest of her life. One early example was when she was 12 years old and suffered an attack of guilt and shame after a nun at St Finbar's School told the class Saint Maria Goretti who died as a martyr, rather than agree to a man's request for sex. Maria Goretti died from injuries received when the man beat her into unconsciousness and raped her. As the nun who told the story and praised the courage and virtue of the young woman, Gwen felt that she too should have fought off her teenage relative's sexual advances in her home. Her guilt seeped deeper and deeper into her subconscious and distorted her attitudes to male and female relations.[17] In those days female fulfilment was to marry well, be a mother and raise a family. Gwen showed no interest in this journey when her peers sought boyfriends and teenage gossip began about 'Who liked who.'

Anne, Brian, Gwen Nell and Barbara out for the day

Gwen was a high achiever, keen on study, reading and sport. In 1938 she completed her Merit Certificate (8th Grade/Year 8). She was dux of her class and captain of the St Finbar's basketball team. She was a strong, determined leader with much promise. Gwen recalls:

> I remember we were to play St Kevin's College at Ormond. We missed the bus. I walked the team all the way up North Road to Ormond from Hawthorn Road. We kept a fair pace and the team was exhausted when we arrived. We lost. I worried about that for weeks, feeling that it was my fault. Actually, our Sports Master was really responsible. He panicked us into thinking that if we were late we would have to forfeit the game.

Disappointment and lost opportunity followed Gwen's success at St Finbar's. Despite her academic success, and sporting and leadership ability,

Gwen did not go on to complete a secondary education. Gwen remembers Bob and Nell telling her that they did not have sufficient money to send her to the local Catholic College at Gardenvale. Gwen's sister, Barbara, believes that her parents would not have done this to Gwen. She contends that 12 year old Gwen, who loved school, study and sport, decided to enrol at Hassett's Ladies Business College to complete a secretarial course in order to earn money. Gwen's recollections appear to be closer to the truth. Bob and Nell may have been struggling to provide for and educate five growing children after the financial disaster of the investment in the Healsville guesthouse. It may have been attractive to have Gwen earn a small wage and contribute to the household budget.

Gwen completed the course at Hassett's successfully and just before her 14th birth day began her first job as a clerical assistant at the Royal Melbourne Golf Club. She found working life monotonous and repetitive. Being young, she was given only menial tasks and had no responsibility. Gwen gave her pay each week to Nell. She grew to regret not being given the opportunity to complete her secondary education as her siblings progressed to secondary education as family finances improved.

Not one to dwell on her circumstances, Gwen developed into a vibrant and confident young teenager. She played tennis, basketball and rode horses. Her friend, Peg Fitzgerald, recalled:

> During our teen years, all of us used to meet at the various church halls for weekly YCW (Young Christian Workers) and NCGM (National Catholic Girls Movement) dances. We had a circuit around all the nearby parishes. Perhaps it was because I waged a constant battle with freckles, particularly on my nose, that I remember Gwen's beautiful olive skin. She was also a 'snazzy' dresser and cut a lovely figure around the dance floor.
>
> But then our lives were literally shattered by the commencement of World War 2. Our fathers and uncles and brothers and friends had to join the Services.

The war closed one door and opened another for Gwen. The manager of the Royal Melbourne Golf Club retrenched her to save her meagre salary within a few weeks of the declaration of war in September 1939. Many club members joined the Services and there was petrol rationing. Fewer people played golf, so the club had to reduce its costs. Bob used his cycling contacts to arrange a job for Gwen in the General Accessories section of Malvern Star bicycles. Older now and no longer relegated to menial office work, Gwen was ambitious to improve her circumstances and soon proved her value. After several weeks she was promoted to become the secretary to the company accountant.

Gwen (right), with friends, probably at Malvern Star

While the War had created an unexpected opportunity for Gwen, the family had to cope with the departure of Bob who 'answered the bugle call'. Emulating many of his male relatives in the First World War, he joined up and embarked with the Sixth Division for the Middle East on Christmas Day 1940, sending back a private soldier's pay and leaving Nell to take care of their five children.

Billy Allsop, Nell's brother, who had already been in the Royal Australian Navy for several years, sailed to the Middle East as a member of the crew of HMAS *Parramatta*. He had converted to Catholicism in order to marry Margaret 'Peggie' McCurry, who had a child, Mary Edna, and then moved home to Christchurch, New Zealand, while Billy sailed to war. He would never see his young wife and daughter again. Peggie remarried after the war and had a large family.

Like his uncles who were also exuberant Aussies, Billy was a patriot, with a witty, vulgar and gregarious character. He is mentioned several times in HMAS *Parramatta's* history. Reportedly, the Governor of South Australia, Sir Malcolm Barclay-Harvey, who was reviewing the ship's crew in June 1940, asked him, 'Do you think you will be ready for whatever you may meet?' He sprang to attention and, presumably in loud affirmation, replied 'Ready in every respect, sir.' [18]

Billy Allsop was the Yeoman of Signals, responsible for *Parramatta's* communications. Though he had responded positively on behalf of every member of *Parramatta's* crew, the ship itself was ill-prepared for modern maritime operations against the well-prepared ships of the German fleet, especially the infamous U Boat submarines, as well as German dive bombers and other aircraft fitted with torpedoes. By Christmas 1940 *Parramatta* was involved in the contest for dominance of the waters of the Mediterranean. On Christmas Day Billy had festooned the masthead and yardarms with a 'Merry Christmas' banner and had flown, 'full battle ensigns, Australian and White'.[19]

On 24 June 1941 *Parramatta* was in action under German aerial attack. After the day dawned 'fine, clear and hot with a smooth seas', HMS *Auckland* was in station ahead of a convoy and *Parramatta* was astern of a fuel ship, both ships zig-zagging to make it hard for U Boats to torpedo them. The first 'stick of bombs' dropped at 8.40 am from reconnaissance aircraft, straddling but not hitting *Parramatta*. German torpedo aircraft followed. After a close call from one torpedo failed to hit *Parramatta*, *Auckland* was not so lucky.

After a large formation of German Stuka dive bombers arrived from the south-east later in the afternoon, 32 attacked *Auckland* and 16 attacked

Parramatta, diving from 14,000 feet. Both ships 'opened with the heaviest barrage their guns could give'. At 5 50 pm several bombs hit *Auckland* and, in it death throes, the mortally wounded out-of-control ship almost collided with *Parramatta*. Despite her own possible needs if hit, *Parramatta* sent her life saving boats and gear to save members of *Auckland's* crew. As *Auckland* sank with heavy loss to its crew, another German attack arrived to finish off *Parramatta*. Her Captain reported,

> *Parramatta* was embarrassed with men in the water round the screws and could not at once go ahead. The attack caught me when the ship was gathering speed. [German aircraft] machine-gunned *Auckland* men in the water, but happily did little harm. ... Then the swine went low over the men in the water and machine-gunned them. I have never felt so angry in my life.

Parramatta survived this second wave of attacks, but 'the sky became alive with aircraft' that evening ... [and] the air seemed so full of shrieking and diving planes that it was impossible to count them'.[20] The history reported:

> Throughout the action, Allsop, Yeoman of Signals, fought his machine-gun on the bridge magnificently. The men afterwards joked that as he fought his gun so fast his flying shells were more dangerous than bomb splinters. He swung his gun to each new attack with fierce concentration and lurid invitations to the enemy to come on, you so and so's![21]

For his bravery during this engagement, Billy Allsop, was awarded the Distinguished Service Medal on 8 January 1942.[22] An award he would not receive in person. In the early hours of November 1941 while escorting a convoy, German submarine U559 launched a torpedo into *Parramatta* causing the ship's magazine to explode. The ship rolled rapidly to starboard and sank within minutes. Acting Commander, Jefferson Walker, had time to order the crew to abandon ship but only about a third of the crew was able to escape, so quick was the sinking.

The other escort ship in the convoy, HMS *Avon Vale*, managed to rescue 21 men despite being some way off at the time of the attack.

Tragically, many of those who survived the sinking perished at sea despite the efforts of *Avon Vale's* crew. Three other survivors made it to shore and were found by advancing British troops. But Billy Allsop was not one of the survivors. He perished with 138 members of the ship's company despite spending some time after the sinking clinging to 'an Oropesa float which had been fitted with lifelines'. [23] Billy's death saddened the family and increased Nell's and her children's anxiety for Bob's safety.

Billy Allsop in his navy uniform

Gwen's Grandmother May was shattered by the death of her only son. She became deeply depressed. Several weeks later, she filled her bath with water, drank a bottle of Lysol disinfectant and lay in the water until she lost consciousness and drowned. Nell's sister, Val, discovered her mother's body and called Nell at Ward Street. Gwen was shocked and stunned when Nell rang her at work and hysterically screamed down the telephone that May was dead.

The loss of Billy and May within a few weeks of each other crushed the Allsop and O'Meara families. Broken by May's suicide, her husband, Bill, came to live at Ward Street with his daughter, Nell, and her children. He was inconsolable and virtually unemployable. Gwen remembers his profound sadness weighed heavily on her. She loved and adored her gentle Granny May. The circumstances of her death deeply shocked and confused her. In those days, suicide by a family member brought public shame. The Catholic and Protestant churches deemed suicide to be a sin against God's Law. May's suicide became a family secret. The story was to be that May had died in her sleep. Such was the shame, May was not afforded a church funeral service and she was buried without public notices.

Meanwhile, Bob had enlisted on 21 June 1940 been posted to the 3rd Australian Army Ordnance Field Park (OFP) (redesignated 2/3 OFP in 1942). He left for the Middle East on 26 December 1940 graded as a 'Group III Storeman TMT' and returned to Australia on 22 March 1942 before deploying to New Guinea on 20 February 1943 after months at the Atherton Tablelands, Queensland. He returned to Australia on 30 March 1944 suffering from dyspepsia. After medical down-grading, he joined the New Guinea Details Depot in Port Moresby. He embarked from Port Moresby on *SS Ormiston* on 28 March 1944 and disembarked in Townsville on 30 March. He spent some time in the 2nd/6thArmy General Hospital and was diagnosed with rheumatic polyarthritis before discharge from the Royal Park personnel depot on 22 September 1945. His records show that he completed 1,919 days of effective service and served overseas for 707 days rising to the rank of Warrant Officer Class Two. His family saw him for 15 days from 21 November until 6 December 1942. He never spoke of his service in the Second World War.

By Gwen's 17th birthday the emotional cost of keeping May's suicide a secret and maintaining family appearances had added to her personal feelings of guilt and shame emanating from the incident of sexual abuse. Nell leaned on Gwen for emotional support, but with no-one to share her own feelings, Gwen grieved alone and felt burdened by Nell's neediness and the demands of her siblings. Once again a challenging situation prompted her to make an important decision. On her 18th birthday in January 1943, Gwen enlisted in the newly raised Women's Royal Australian Navy Service.

Bob, in uniform, says farewell to his family–Gwen in her mid-teens

Corporal Robert (Bob) O'Meara

Gwen's enlistment upset Nell who felt that Bob was doing enough for the war effort, and that her family had endured too much heartache already. Ignoring her mother's entreaties for her to change her mind, Gwen left a few weeks later to begin her basic training on the HMAS *Cerberus* at Mornington Peninsula. Brian wrote later:

> It was with a mixture of pride and sadness that I saw my sister walk into our home in the neatness of the uniform of the Senior Service. The lump in my throat was the product of a fear that Gwen might go to a war zone, be at risk, and maybe not return.

Over the next three years Gwen worked as a tele-typist at HMAS *Cerberus*, at Navy Headquarters in Melbourne and finally at HMAS *Harman* in Canberra. Peg Russell, one of Gwen's supervisors, remembered her as 'a very nice girl', 'middle of the road', 'no rocking of boats, or odd behaviour', 'not snobby or bitchy like some of the others'. Every week Gwen sent her mother money to help meet the family's financial commitments.

In January 1946 Gwen turned 21years. She was popular, enjoying a wide circle of friends from East Brighton and the Navy. Gwen was friendly with everyone. Life in the Navy has developed her into an independent, confident young woman who no longer had any misconceptions about 'the birds and the bees', but eschewed close relationships with men

Gwen in Navy rig

Gwen front and centre with her navy cohort

In 1946 Gwen left the Navy and returned to live at home and work at back at Malvern Star. At home, things had changed dramatically. The war years had been a great strain on Nell. Her husband had been away for five years, her mother and brother had died in tragic circumstances, and her father was living at home, deaf and heart broken. With five children, Nell had had to survive on a Warrant Officer's pay. To their credit, the older children stepped up to help their mother and earned money doing odd jobs for neighbours.

The war changed Bob forever. He had served with an Ordnance Field Park, a supply unit, rising from the rank of private soldier to Regimental Sergeant Major. Bob was a different father and husband after the war. Like many returned service personnel, he was preoccupied and distant from his family for some time. In their turn, Nell and the children had grown independent and self-sufficient. He found it difficult to return to his roles as a father and husband quickly after five years away. Gwen perceived that Bob and Nell's marriage went through a major crisis in the year or so following his return. Bob was no longer as fun loving, or as family oriented as he had been before the war. He went about his duties to the family quietly, dutifully and purposefully, but keeping his own counsel. Gwen found the home environment tense and uncomfortable.

Gwen's relationship with Nell had become difficult after returning home. Nell treated her as a dutiful daughter who had to help around the house and keep her company. She also sought a great deal of emotional support from Gwen while her relationship with Bob was readjusting after his return. She needed Gwen's companionship. But Gwen did not share Nell's view of her family obligations. She also felt that a gap had developed between herself and her brothers and sisters while she was in the Navy. She began looking to change her circumstances.

Joining her sister, Barbara, Gwen began training as a nurse at St Vincent's Hospital. She moved from home and lived at the hospital. But after contracting a serious virus in 1947 from drinking contaminated milk, which kept her from work for three months, Gwen could not keep up with the physical demands of nursing on her return, and decided to leave.

Gwen in her St Vincent's Hospital nursing outfit

Barbara in her St Vincent's Hospital nursing outfit

Gwen found herself at a cross road after recovering from her illness. She was unemployed, but with excellent typing, short hand and clerical skills. She was not having a happy time at home and her failure to become a nurse contrasted with her sister Barbara's competence and confidence. Her father, Bob, was distant and occasionally difficult as he struggled to engage his children after five years away and a difficult adjustment to suburban life in Melbourne. Her mother Nell needed Gwen's support, but she and her eldest daughter had not formed the mutually respectful relationship that should be the basis of domestic teamwork.

In 1948, aged 23 years, Gwen decided to leave her family, her home town and Australia for a working holiday and overseas adventure. The first step was to get work away from Melbourne and save money for the onward journey. She secured a job as a tele-typist with Trans Australia Airlines in Hobart, her intention being to work for a few months, save money, and then travel to Europe. She planned to satisfy a long held desire to travel to overseas places where others had served during the war.

Marital Years 1951-1959

Gwen settled into her work as a tele-typist and enjoyed the social scene in Hobart. In 1950 she met Keith Breen, a freight clerk with Trans Australia Airlines, who was also a keen member of the Sandy Bay football team and a talented musician who played clarinet and saxophone. After several months of courting they announced their engagement and nominated October 10, 1951 as the date for their wedding at St Finbar's Church. The O'Meara and Breen families gathered in formal 'black tie' attire for a Roman Catholic wedding ceremony. Brian and Barbara made up the bridal party. Keith's parents, Jack and Beatrice (nee Pearce) had six children: Barry (22), Keith (21), Gerald (20), Kevin (18), Janice (6) and Lorraine (3).

Violet (Beatrice) and Jack with their son Keith and his sisters Lorraine and Janette, probably on the block in Sandy Bay

Gwen with her Tasmanian beau
Keith Breen

Gwen and Keith
at their St Finbar's
wedding

Gwen dressed up and
out and about

Keith and Gwen honeymooned at Lorne in Victoria. Afterwards they returned to Hobart and temporarily moved in with Keith's parents while Keith and his brothers built a house on a block of land in Sandy Bay on the lower slopes of Mt William. Keith kept frequent contact with his parents, Jack and Beatrice, and his three brothers and two sisters.

These were not happy times for Gwen. Beatrice was an interfering and judgemental woman. It was difficult for Gwen to build her relationship with Keith when members of his family were present most of the time. Keith was immature and did not assert himself with his parents on behalf of his new bride. Indeed, he continued his life largely uninterrupted by his marital commitments. Gwen remembers him spending more time at the football club, golf club or rehearsing and playing with his band than with her. She did not participate in the socialising and heavy drinking associated with Keith's social scene. They were growing apart from the beginning.

Her situation was further complicated by an unexpected pregnancy. Nine months and ten days after her wedding day, Gwen gave birth to a son, Robert, at Mount Calvary Hospital in Hobart. Gwen learned the hard way that the Rhythm Method of birth control recommended by her church was not reliable.

Keith (right) with band members and friends

While he was not the most devoted husband, Keith was nonetheless an industrious and ambitious young man, keen to provide a home for his family. In 1953, he, his father and three brothers dug foundations and built a three-bedroom house in Lower Sandy Bay that was later to become one of the most prestigious Derwent riverside suburbs of Hobart.

Soon after the house was completed, Gwen put on a party for Keith's friends, most of whom were musicians and footballers. This was her first taste of the hedonistic lifestyle Keith favoured. She was revolted by their heavy drinking and sexual promiscuity. A non-smoker and non-drinker, as well as a devoted Christian, Gwen was already at odds with her husband and his friends who smoked drank and gratified themselves sexually. She never again hosted a party for Keith's friends at her home. Her focus turned to Robert, a lively, fair-haired toddler, and then to baby, Peter, who was born in May 1954.

In early 1955 Keith and Gwen purchased a mixed business in Moonah near the Hobart city centre that were often called 'Milk Bars' in those days. They decided that Peter would be their last child, and sold the house at Lower Sandy Bay and moved into accommodation at their shop. They looked forward to a prosperous future building their small corner store providing fresh bread, milk, fruit and other groceries to the local community. While Keith worked as a clerk in the Tasmanian Hydro Electricity Commission, Gwen ran the shop.

*Keith holding a young Robert John and Gwen holding newly born
Peter Francis Breen, on a visit to Melbourne*

Running a mixed business and looking after two toddlers required energy, organisation and commitment. Gwen threw herself into her role as business woman, wife and mother with vigour and determination for the next year and a half. Unfortunately, she was not getting sufficient help from Keith, who directed most of his time and talent to pleasing himself. When he was not working, he divided his time between Australian Rules football, golf, music and drinking. He played football for the Hydro Electricity Commission team in the winter and tried to fit in a round or two of golf on fine weather weekends.

Keith was an accomplished and naturally gifted musician. He formed a swing dance band with friends in the early 1950s and played Glen Miller style music at the Hobart City Hall on Saturday nights. He became a show business personality in Hobart, occasionally playing with the Tasmanian ABC Band on radio. Keith also spent most Sundays including evenings playing at jam sessions with musicians from around Hobart in their homes. After performances and jam sessions, they had parties with their wives and girlfriends. Gwen never went to these after-parties. She lived in a parallel world to her husband taking care of Robert and Peter at home.

Keith's sporting and musical interests, as well as an active, separate social life left little time for Gwen and the boys. Gwen preferred a quieter lifestyle at home anyway. During her years in the Navy she had avoided the 'party scene' and was well aware of the dangers of women drinking heavily in the company of men. She did not drink and was critical of the drunken and loose lifestyle of Keith's fellow musicians, their wives and girlfriends.

In 1955 Gwen fell pregnant again after returning to the Rhythm Method of birth control. This upset her plans to continue working in the mixed business. She could not run the business, rear two demanding and energetic young boys, prepare meals for the family and keep house while she was pregnant. Keith and Gwen decided to sell up. Gwen battled on running the business for two more months until new owners took over. She was lonely and exhausted. When she asked for more support from Keith, and implored him to spend more time with the boys, he became frustrated and angry. Gwen was disheartened by his ambivalence to family life, and concerned that he was leading a quasi-bachelor life within his hedonistic social circle.

There were other tensions. Gwen regarded sex as a duty she had to perform as a wife, and not a pleasure for herself. In the early years of their marriage she and Keith were willing but ignorant love makers. Despite becoming more informed during her years in the Navy and while training as a nurse, she felt that being sexually abused at seven years of age had left her inhibited and anxious as a partner.

Gwen and Keith argued about her sexual inhibitions. Keith made Gwen feel inadequate and mocked her lack of responsiveness. He compared her performance unfavourably to the descriptions of female sexuality he had read in books and was possibly experiencing with the young women attracted to his band. His taunts only reinforced the hurt and guilt Gwen carried with her from her humiliating childhood experience.

Over time Keith took out his dissatisfaction with his family responsibilities and Gwen's repeated reminders to be a better father on Robert, who sensed the tension between his parents and acted up. Keith would come home drunk and, when Robert acted up after being ignored, Keith would take off his belt and beat him. At four years of age these beatings were forever etched in Robert's memories, especially at bath time at night when they were delivered while he cowered naked and wet in the bathroom.

The shouting between his parents while Gwen tried to dissuade Keith from delivering these beatings seared into Robert's subconscious and influenced his behaviour in ways that would become serious later in his life when betrayal, rejection and humiliation would arouse intense feelings of anxiety and anger amidst bouts of depression, originating from being abused during his early years.

In late 1956 Gwen decided to spend some time with her family in Melbourne in the latter months of her pregnancy with another child. Part of this time would coincide with Keith's long service leave. She planned to stay at a hotel in Lancefield with her parents and brother, Brian, who was the licensee. Gwen looked forward to the support of her family and the opportunity to relax among caring relatives.

In early January 1957, a few days before her 32nd birthday, Gwen, and the boys flew to Melbourne. Her father, Bob, picked them up and drove them to Lancefield, one hours drive north of Melbourne. Keith joined Gwen and the boys a few weeks later.

Bob and Nell's move from East Brighton to Lancefield had been for commercial as well as family reasons. Brian needed help running the hotel. Bob and Nell decided that by living and working at the pub, they could see more of their favourite son. But running the country pub had more 'downs' than 'ups' for Bob, Nell and Brian. The long hours for modest financial returns, the cold climate, coping with difficult clientele, and the restricted trading hours kept Bob and Brian very busy, and sent Nell's health into decline.

The arrival of Keith, Gwen and the boys was welcome but added to the pressures at Lancefield. Keith helped Brian in the bar, and assisted when fights broke out. Gwen took care of the kids and helped Nell with domestic duties. On April 5, 1957 she gave birth to a daughter, Helen, at the Lancefield Hospital. After three months at Lancefield, Gwen and Keith returned to Hobart with the boys and their new baby girl.

Gwen with her two young boys at Lancefield

Keith decided to build a house further up the slopes of Sandy Bay in Red Chapel Avenue, one of the most picturesque locations in Hobart. The family lived in a rented house while their new home was being built. Gwen hoped that Keith would spend more time with her and the children after they settled in. But Keith returned to the lifestyle that had put so much pressure on their marriage before going to Lancefield. He worked hard and played hard. He was promoted at work and his career seemed to be taking off. He formed a three-piece band and played every night of the week except Sundays at the Wrest Point Hotel. On Sundays he played and drank with other musicians.

Gwen felt that she and the kids 'cramped his style'. He either ignored or rebuffed the understandable demands for attention from his sons. His drinking and tiredness led him to physically abuse them if he was the least bit annoyed with their behaviour. Gwen tried to protect them from their father, but her interventions led to more conflict. Robert recalled:

> There are mixed memories from this period. I have some images of my father as a happy-go-lucky person giving us piggybacks and wrestling on the floor. I also have very unpleasant memories of him taking off his belt and using it to thrash me vigorously around the legs while he held me by one arm. Peter used to get the same treatment. I think his worst effort was belting both of us when we were naked in the bathroom. I am sure we probably did something to annoy him, but I felt that being beaten while naked was one of the ultimate humiliations in anyone's life. He used to slap Helen, even though she was only a baby, when he could not stop her crying. Even then I thought this was a cowardly act. I felt great anger and fear.

By the end of the year Gwen and Keith's marriage was in crisis. Ahead were months of emotional turmoil. Keith spent more time away from home, either on the golf course, with his band, or partying with his mates and their wives and female companions. Gwen was alone with six year old, Robert, and four year old, Peter, a two year old, Helen.

Keith was a sexual bully, a husband who did not like 'No' for an answer. The Roman Catholic Church-approved Rhythm Method could not work under these circumstances and failed Gwen again. She fell pregnant with her fourth child. Keith turned down Gwen's offer to have a hysterectomy to end her fertility after this child. Gwen committed herself reluctantly to artificial contraception to prevent further pregnancies in contravention of the directives from the Roman Catholic Church. Too late for her fourth pregnancy in seven years. Baby Annette was on her way.

What Gwen didn't know at the time was that Keith had begun an affair with an 18-year-old girl who also worked at the Hydro Electricity Commission. She went to see him play music and joined in the drinking sessions after his band had finished for the night. One weekend Gwen insisted that she be given a break from the children. She ordered Keith to stay home and look after them for a few hours. On her return she found Keith's work colleague, Jan, in the house. Gwen was immediately suspicious of his relationship with the teenager. Her instincts told her to do something to discourage Keith's interest in Jan. However, unexpected events overtook her.

Late in 1959 Keith told Gwen that he was moving to Queensland for a year to follow an opportunity to become a television performer. He said he could not afford to take Gwen and the children with him. Bewildered by this sudden announcement and with few options available to her, Gwen informed her parents that after the birth of her next child in December she would be coming to Melbourne to live until Keith's return. Keith's parents, Jack and Beatrice, offered no assistance to Gwen and her children, seemingly leaving the consequences of their son's decision to move to Queensland to be sorted out by Gwen's family.

Bob and Nell offered Gwen all the support they could muster when she and the children came over. Gwen hoped that Keith would return to Melbourne to be with his children and forego his lifestyle in Hobart after returning from Queensland. If his career move was successful, Gwen hoped that he would call his family to be with him in Brisbane. She did not want him to go back to Hobart and renew contact with Jan, whom she suspected was becoming closer to her husband, or his mates, who condoned his lifestyle away from his family.

In December 1959 Gwen gave birth to a second daughter, Annette, whom she named after her favourite teacher at St Finbar's Primary School, Sister Annette. She had already arranged to fly to Melbourne as soon as she and Annette were ready to travel. This was a very sad time in Gwen's life. Keith saved one last insult for her and violated the sanctity of her home before she left. She arrived home with Annette from the hospital to find that Keith had allowed one of his older musician mates—a grandfather with a family in Launceston—to sleep with his young girlfriend in their bed. Gwen was outraged that Keith had allowed her home and marital bed to be violated by what she considered to be a lecherous old man and his tart.

Keith farewelled his family at Hobart airport and wept. His mother had died some years before and his father was interstate, so this was a private, very sad family event. Cradling Annette in her arms, Gwen shed her own tears. Soon to be 35 and with four children under the age of eight years, she was now being deserted by her husband, whom she suspected was having an affair with a teenager.

Gwen knew that Keith was not a good husband or father, but hoped, somehow, that he would grow up and meet his obligations to her and his children. Adding to her feelings of abandonment was her perception that Bob and Nell disapproved of her decision to move to Melbourne and not

Gwen with her four children, her mother Nell (left)
brother Brian O'Meara and sister Anne.

await Keith's return in their home in Sandy Bay. Bob, Nell and her brothers and sisters were loyal to her, but she assessed that they were also questioning her judgment and her competence as a wife and mother. This perception compounded her anger and also deepened her unacknowledged but destructive feelings of shame and guilt from her childhood. Gwen was angry and alone—an abandoned lioness with her four cubs. And she was fierce. Her children came first, her pride and anger second, and everyone else could suit themselves. She wanted to fight back from misfortune and maintain her independence.

While looking for somewhere to live, Gwen and the kids stayed with her parents in Bay Street, North Brighton. Bob and Nell did everything they could to make Gwen and the children comfortable and welcome. Robert recalled:

> I remember this short time at Bay Street as being one where we received much love and kindness. Grandfather [Bob] had a light-blue Vanguard panel van with upholstery that had a leathery, tobacco smell in the mornings when it was first opened up. He used to drive Peter and I to the Gardenvale Catholic Primary School each morning. He gave us each a small white lolly bag full of peanuts before we got out of the van. He touched me with his kindness. He did not speak to us very much, but this simple gift of peanuts each morning showed that he cared. He was a man to be judged more by his actions than by his words.

Within a few months Gwen bought a three-bedroom weatherboard house at 73 Regent Street, Elsternwick. She enrolled her sons at the nearby St Joseph's Catholic Primary School. Small amounts of money from Keith helped to make ends meet while she nursed her new baby.

Gwen hoped that Keith would return, behave more responsibly, save their marriage and be a father to his children. By day, she was assertive and independent. By night her children heard her crying alone in bed.

Break-Up and Breakdown Years 1960-1965

For Gwen, 1960 was a pivotal and disastrous year. The future was full of unknowns and uncertainties. She felt isolated in Elsternwick. Keith, still in Queensland, only contacted her occasionally. Bob and Nell continued to assist Brian to run the pub in Lancefield. They did their best to provide support to Gwen but it was difficult for them during this period to keep in touch with her and the children. Nell's health was a major family concern as well. She was not happy living at the pub and the physical work was wearing her down.

Towards the end of the year Keith moved to Melbourne from Queensland. Gwen insisted that 12 months was long enough and had ordered him back. Both his parents and Gwen's parents also put pressure on for him to return. He moved into the house at Elsternwick and there was an attempt at reconciliation. By this time Regent Street had deteriorated into an untidy, chaotic place. Gwen did her best once a week to restore some order to the house but it was an impossible job with four children. Robert and Peter were running wild and fought incessantly.

Keith's return led to further wildness as the boys tried to gain attention and ascertain what was going on with their parents. Keith returned to beating Robert whom he appeared to take a particular dislike. For his part,

Robert recalls wanting a father's love and attention, but at the same time hating him for his violence and attitude to Gwen, and deeply resenting his violence towards him. This love/hate conflict with his father was damaging for an eight year old.

After a few weeks Keith moved out. Gwen had fought with him over his refusal to take Robert and Peter on a holiday to Hobart. The three elder children watched as their parents yelled and punched each other. Dark blue bruises remained on Gwen's upper arms and shoulders for several days to remind her and the children of this dramatic altercation and his angry departure.

Despite this incident, Gwen still begged Keith to return and to be a father to his children. He did visit occasionally and took the family out, or stayed for a night. He was preoccupied and evasive. These outings were tense and sad. Everyone knew that the marriage was not working. Peter remembered:

> Robert was older and more aware. I think he must have missed his father's care and affection more. But for me, two years younger, life was more of a blur with only a few more dramatic events recalled in later life. I remember Hobart and a harshness in my father, particularly if Robert and I disturbed him early in the morning. I remember my mother regularly waiting up for him into the early hours.
>
> There were also happy times doing things that kids do, such as collecting tadpoles and watching them grow. In Melbourne, at age four, I do not recall missing my father in Queensland. But I remember the conflict at 73 Regent Street when he returned. I remember the shock I felt seeing my mother's bruises from one particular fight and I still have a vivid picture of them in my mind. I can see my hand reaching for my father's keys on the red carpet in the hallway. I was not sad to see him take the keys from my hand and leave.

During this time there were several open discussions between Keith and Gwen and Keith's father, Jack. Gwen recalled that at one of these discussions, Jack with his head in his hands and weeping, threatened to cut Keith from his inheritance if he did not return to his family and try to make the marriage work. Gwen also started to cry. Jack looked up with a sneer and said, 'That's a great way to try and keep a husband.' Gwen felt that deep down Jack blamed her for the state of her marriage and was really on his son's side. Jack did not know that Keith was lying about why he would not meet his responsibilities as a husband and father.

Finally, Keith summoned the courage to tell Gwen why he had moved to Queensland and what had gone on there. Arriving home one night at 2am, after playing in a band, he got into bed and despondently told her the story. Twelve months before, he had decided to take his young girlfriend, Jan, to Queensland because she was pregnant and he did not have the courage to tell her parents, his parents or Gwen. He had made up the story about being offered the job on television. Jan gave birth to a baby boy, Gary, a few months before Keith returned to Melbourne. Jan and Gary had travelled with him, and he had been seeing them regularly during the parent-directed reconciliation period with Gwen. He concluded by telling Gwen that he had now made up his mind to leave her and the children permanently so that he could set up a home with Jan and baby, Gary.

After months of anxiety, loneliness and uncertainty, Keith's confession totally swamped Gwen's senses. She recalled 'blacking out'. Eventually she became conscious that she was crawling around the floor of the bedroom in the dark, whimpering and sobbing. The final realisation that her marriage was over kicked the fight out of her. She could not speak. She was numb, empty and devastated. He departed without another word, leaving her alone, weeping in the dark.

During the tearful, sleepless hours before dawn, Gwen resolved to make a new start and get on with bringing up her children without the support of her husband. She fed on a fierce, burning anger at his betrayal. She would show the world that she was not going to be a victim, and that her children were not going to suffer because their father had abandoned them. However Keith's departure did hurt the children. Gwen recalled:

Robert was in bed one morning and I could see by the look in his sad blue eyes that he was suffering. I said, "You love your father, don't you?" The look on his face was enough for me to know that he knew I understood his suffering. Helen was upset when Keith left and cried. I told her to go to sleep, but she woke in an hour, sobbing. I did my best to comfort her.

Gwen arranged for Robert, Peter and Helen to spend the Christmas holidays in 1960 with her sister, Barbara, and her family. Jack and Barbara owned a farm in Litchfield in North West Victoria. This was a generous gesture by Barbara. Her husband, Jack, was harvesting wheat—his family's livelihood—from dawn until dusk. The threat of fire sweeping through the crops was high, and everyone in the district kept a look out, taking their fire fighting equipment to put out fires on any neighbouring properties. Jack and Barbara had four children of their own to manage over this busy and commercially vital period.

Robert Breen and cousin Kate Melican at the Litchfield farm

With the older kids taken care of, Gwen put Annette into child care and went out looking for a job. Fortunately a receptionist position within walking distance of Regent Street came up with a local solicitor in Glenhuntly Road. By the time the boys and Helen returned from Litchfield after Christmas, things had begun to look up. Gwen charged into each day; organising Robert and Peter for school, and Helen and Annette for childcare, preparing breakfast and cutting lunches, sending Robert and Peter out the door for the walk to St Joseph's and driving Helen and Annette to childcare.

Several days after Keith left, Gwen had sought help from Father Maurice, a local Catholic priest, who had been recommended to her. His counselling was disastrous. After Gwen told him her story, he stated that Keith had lost respect for her because she had used artificial contraception and she was not doing her best to achieve a reconciliation. He instructed her to get back with Keith, to find out what he really wanted from her and to save the marriage.[24] Gwen wrote later:

> It wasn't just what he said, but how he said it. I burst into tears and asked him if he had a tissue. He said, 'No, I haven't.' in a voice which implied he wouldn't give me one, [even] if he had it. I was utterly devastated. Many years later I went to a lecture and in his talk he said exactly the same thing [about Catholic women using artificial contraception and losing the respect of their husbands]—I nearly fell of the chair.

Father Maurice ignored Gwen's brokenness from Keith's violence towards her and her children and his abandonment of them for a teenager whom he had got pregnant and now lived with out of wedlock. Rather than listening and trying to bring about healing, he deepened Gwen's feelings of guilt and shame. She wrote later, 'I feel that this counsellor [Father Maurice] ... stripped me of my dignity as a person.'

There was more humiliation to come. Later that same week Keith returned to pack his belongings, accompanied by Jan's father whom Gwen had never met. This man questioned Gwen aggressively about why she would not give Keith a divorce. She replied that she did not know that he even wanted one. Jan's father did not seem to believe her. Clearly, Keith had been lying to him about Gwen as a person and how his marriage worked. He had most likely convinced him that he was not marrying his daughter, Jan, and legitimising her son because Gwen would not give him a divorce. One can only guess the other lies Keith may have told Jan's father to justify his infidelity.

Gwen's humiliation deepened further when her workplace became an additional source of stress. The solicitor's friendliness turned into sexual harassment. He began by brushing against her and occasionally touching her lightly. His intentions were obvious. This was the last thing Gwen wanted or needed. She was torn by the need to keep her job and her determination not to succumb to his persistent physical advances.

After refusing to go out and drink with her predatory employer several times, he became more and more irritable and critical of her work. One night he arrived at Regent Street drunk, demanding to be let in. He worked his way around the house looking for a way to enter. Gwen was terrified. She feared that he might hurt her and the children. She called the police and told him they were coming. He left, but not before leaving Gwen and Robert deeply fearful of his intentions. Once again, Robert felt impotent and cowardly in face of the aggression of a man towards him and his mother.

The next day at work Gwen tried to reason with the solicitor and dissuade him from further harassment, especially by visiting her home and unsettling her children. She told him over and over again that she did not want to socialise with him. She was desperately trying to keep her job and to stop his harassment. In the end the solicitor's wife intervened. She insisted that Gwen be sacked because her husband could not control himself. With no notice, the solicitor told her to pack up and leave. Once again Gwen was again a victim of male treachery and betrayal.

Unemployed and with four children to care for, Gwen was soon under acute financial pressure. Keith was not sending sufficient money to pay the mortgage at Regent Street, or to take care of other bills. She did not want to ask her parents or her brothers and sister for any more money. They had already been generous, as well as providing clothing and other items for the kids. The local St Vincent de Paul Society had also been helpful. She now had to find another job without a reference from her previous employer. She did not want to talk about the circumstances of her dismissal. Who would have believed her anyway?

The worry and uncertainty of trying finding another job put Gwen under extreme emotional pressure. Her self-esteem had hit rock bottom, an accumulation of Keith's final abandonment, Jan's father's accusations, Father Maurice's destructive advice, and finally, her sacking from the solicitor's office. For the first time in her life, Gwen did not have the self-confidence to get a job. She applied for six jobs, but knew that she had interviewed poorly. There were no offers for this broken woman.

At home, the boys were becoming more and more unruly. They fought with each other constantly, misbehaved at school, and spent long periods of time after school roaming the streets of Elsternwick. Helen and Annette, only toddlers, withdrew into themselves as they tried to cope with their mother's depression and their brothers' delinquency.

Four angelic looking children, but looks can deceive

The pressure on Gwen increased at a time when she needed to concentrate on healing her own hurt, building up her self-esteem and finding a job. Her heart broke as she watched her children suffering and out of control. Robert recalled:

> I was quite independent and feral, apart from the controls exercised on me during school hours by the nuns at St Joseph's, who were ironically called Sisters of Mercy.

There was no mercy for me as they applied rulers to my knuckles during well-deserved but physically and mentally hurtful punishments. Mum was extremely busy and had to spend time tending to Helen and Annette who were still very young. She put me into a cub/scout pack to give me some exposure to discipline and male role models. Much to Mum's chagrin, a female cub leader replaced the male leader soon after I began there. I enjoyed cubs and became a sixer (a leader of six other cubs). Cubs was good for me, but I did not go onto scouts. The initiation period involved humiliating recruits physically and mentally. I was not up to it. I hated being bullied, and did not return after the first night.

I took Mum for granted during this period and regret the extra pressure I put on her because of my behaviour and long absences from home. I was angry, selfish and aggressive. Unfortunately Peter was on the other end of my aggression in those days. I either ignored him or responded violently if I felt provoked. A psychologist would have diagnosed me as reacting badly to the marriage break-up and possibly even mimicking my father's brutality.

Despite her own anxiety and grief, Gwen gave total support to her children during this period. Many years later, on the occasion of her 70th birthday, they wrote to her about their memories of her parenting during these uncertain and difficult times.

Robert:

Mum, you were and are the most comforting person I have ever known. One-to-one you were at your best. I remember many times coming to you to seek reassurance and encouragement when I felt overcome by some hurt I had endured at school, or elsewhere. You made me feel 'special'. Well before the term became popular, you were building the self-esteem of your children—one of the greatest gifts a parent can give, apart from unconditional love. I did not have to seek assurances about your love. I always knew it was there.

Peter:

You battled on to keep the wolf from the door and you did so cheerfully and lovingly. This is all any child can expect.'

Helen:

> I feel as a child I will always remember the times when you would let me into your bed and comfort me from my bad dreams or worries, and you would always warm my feet because you were always warm as toast.

Annette:

> I have a strong memory of a feeling of security and warmth that you gave me. Those times that I climbed into your bed, you were always warm and welcoming. I don't ever remember you saying, 'go away', or 'not now'. You were always there to listen, help or just to cuddle.

After weeks of anxiety and post-interview rejection, Gwen was finally offered a secretarial position in Port Melbourne with General Motors Holden. After that her days were very full. She forced herself to put aside her grief and to get on with being a mother and breadwinner. Her abilities and diligence attracted the attention of senior management. She was soon promoted to a senior secretary's position. Her promotion increased her status at work and gave her a feeling of accomplishment, but it also increased the level of stress in her life. She employed a child minder, also named Gwen, to take care of the kids after school. She was making every possible effort to give them as normal a life as possible. Robert recalled:

> Gwen, the baby-sitter, was a complete disaster. Mum had to sack her after a few weeks when she realised that she was belting me around, denying us food and making us—especially me— more hostile. Despite Mum's best efforts, Peter and I became 'latch key' kids and neighbourhood 'urchins'.

Probably in response to his defiance, Gwen the baby-sitter was particularly cruel to Robert. Encouraged by Gwen to teach Robert to play the piano she injured his fingers systematically when he practiced and missed the correct keys. Needless to say, Robert did not warm to becoming a pianist. Her final humiliation in her cruelty towards Robert was to serve insufficient food at his birthday party to which he had invited several school friends.

Guests and his brother and sisters had to grab for the little food that was brought out begrudgingly. The consequences of this humiliation at the party lasted several weeks afterwards when several of those who had attended mocked Robert in front of others for inviting them to a birthday party where the food ran out.

Four Breen children in front of 73 Regent street, as life was about to take a dramatic turn

Towards the end of 1962 after two horrendous years of betrayal, loss and uncertainty, the stress in Gwen's life began to take its toll. She was meeting everyone else's needs, but her own. The demands on her time and energy grew. Like a pressure cooker ready to burst, her mind was over-heating and psychological cracks began to appear. Her life and her children were out of control, and eventually her mind lost control. Robert, who was nine years old at the time, recalled:

> One morning Mum went silent. She did not respond to our demands—no breakfast, no help with finding our clothes for school. She appeared to be in world of her own. I needed a note for school. She took out a piece of paper and wrote, 'Jesus, Mary and Joseph'. I looked at her and knew that she had lost her mind. I hoped it was temporary and decided to ignore it. I could not face the truth. Deep down my heart was breaking. I walked to school empty and sad. I hoped Mum would be OK

by the time she returned from work. Like the other times I wanted to intervene, such as when my father yelled at her, or the time they were punching each other, I walked away and did nothing. I still feel very guilty about not doing something more for her on that day.'

Peter, who was seven years old at the time, remembered that day:

Robert and I had become self-reliant at a very young age. In our own way we were able to cook and look after ourselves after school, and in the mornings it was much the same. On this morning something was wrong. Mum was not out of bed, and despite our actions, was barely conscious. Nevertheless, Robert and I knew she would not want to be late for work and we helped her up and got her dressed. She seemed to improve and somehow she was able to get to work. We set off for school. It was not really a surprise to find Gran at home after school and that Mum had been taken to hospital. Interestingly, I was not told what kind of hospital, just that my mother was not well and needed a rest.

On that day, 21 November 1962, Gwen had been sent home from work after she was found staring into space while standing near a filing cabinet. While driving home she hallucinated. She stopped the car when she saw a white cloud in the sky and, in her own words, 'heard the voice of Our Lady, the Blessed Virgin Mary, saying that Russia would be saved.' She then drove to her parent's house in Bay Street, Brighton, and repeatedly asked for cups of coffee which she did not drink. In a deeply depressed and psychotic state Gwen told Bob and Nell that her children, 'will soon be going to heaven'. She also said that she was hearing voices telling her to save Russia, presumably from Communism.

After calling their family doctor, Dr John Kenny, to examine Gwen, Bob reluctantly agreed that Gwen had suffered a serious mental breakdown and urgently needed psychiatric help. He drove her to Royal Park Psychiatric Hospital, Carlton. Her admission papers stated:

Admitted PHRP (Psychiatric Hospital Royal Park) 21 November 1962 (by father). Lies in bed staring at the ceiling;

makes vague and obtuse remarks; she is disoriented as to place and time. She said that her children would go to heaven very soon. ... Mother and father alive, both 57.

Two brothers 30, 28; two sisters 33, 32. Patient is the eldest in family [37 years old]. Mother had nervous illness some years ago—nature of illness not known. Maternal Grandmother committed suicide. ... hearing voices, especially that of God. Describes having several hallucinations. ... Silent periods of up to three minutes—frequently blocks and loses train of thought. She discusses almost exclusively her delusional and hallucinatory world. ... Has been a person of above average intellect. Clinical condition: paranoid schizophrenia.

Factors Involved: Desertion by husband leaving her with four young children. She has been working as a secretary for about three years in order to sustain them. Treatment: Electro Convulsive Therapy 3 (times) weekly for three months.

Gwen recalled that fateful day years later.

... On my arrival at the entrance I saw the sign 'Psychiatric Hospital'. I said to myself, 'Dear Lord, just to add to my worries I've gone insane.

Nell visited Gwen at Royal Park on most days. This involved a long trip from Brighton by tram through the busy city centre and back. In those days a closed ward at Royal Park was a disturbing place for anyone not used to being among psychiatrically disturbed people.

For Nell it must have been terrifying because she was a highly-strung person subject to anxiousness. She must have been shocked at Gwen's appearance and behaviour. Strong psychiatric drugs and electro-convulsive therapy transformed Gwen into a zombie. Her eyes were dull and fixed, her face contorted, her teeth yellow and her speech impaired. She walked stiffly in a robot-like fashion and took some time to acknowledge Nell's presence. She was 'hearing voices, especially that of God'.[25]

Two incidents at Royal Park survived in Gwen's memory:

I was asleep and woke up to the sounds of a commotion. There was a patient on the floor with a nurse of rather large proportions sitting on top of her holding her by her hair. Another nurse was kneeling beside the patient trying to give her an injection. The patient was resisting with all her might. I got out of bed, went over and said 'Steady', a word I used to calm my two boys when they were fighting.

All activity stopped. To this day I do not know whether the nurse took advantage of the lull and administered the needle or not. I just trotted back to bed and went to sleep.

... They had music to dance to during some of the organised activities at Royal Park. I asked a little Italian lady to get up with me. She said she could not dance. I insisted. I pointed to the music and then to her ear. She got the message to listen. I took her by the shoulders and pumped them in time with the music and her feet followed. All of a sudden she got into the rhythm of the music. The look on her face was something to behold. I consider that to be one of my lovely moments at Royal Park.

Scenes of mentally disturbed people heavily sedated by drugs and shuffling to and fro meaninglessly were depicted in the film *One flew over the cuckoo's nest*. The sounds of anguish and mania at mental institutions have also been part of several other Hollywood films over the years. While the movie makers have the institutional images right, the challenge remains for Hollywood to capture sights and sounds inside the heads of patients.

Gwen's hallucinations focussed on saving Russia. She recalls:

'... the whole bed began to rock. Then the whole world seemed to be rocking. I felt that the Russians were coming. I rallied the whole world to get into the act and push the Russians back with 'love waves'. I'm not sure what 'love waves' are, but it seemed like a good idea at the time.

I was set to become a charismatic figure sent by God to Russia to convert them from atheism. Our Lady's voice would say over and over again, 'Russia will be saved'. My medical records show that I said I saw this message printed on a cloud while I was driving. [Actually,] I only heard the voice. If I had seen a vision of the Blessed Virgin, I would have really freaked out.

In the early 1960s there was a great deal of ignorance about mental illness in general, and schizophrenia in particular. The situation has not changed significantly since then. Anne Deveson wrote in her book, *Tell me I'm here*, about her family's experience with her son's schizophrenia.

> Schizophrenia still presents medical research with one of its greatest challenges. Much about the illness remains a mystery, but gradually its complexities are being unlocked as advances in technology enable us to record activities of the brain functioning in a variety of ways, and to identify specific differences in brain functioning between those who have the illness and those who do not.
>
> With schizophrenia, fundamental processes in the brain are disturbed, distorting the way a person thinks and experiences the world. Messages are channelled to the wrong responses, like an old fashioned telephone switchboard making faulty connections. Information floods in and overwhelms the brain.
>
> Nobody is yet certain why this malfunctioning occurs. Some kind of vulnerability seems to be built into the system, which may be due to disturbances—genetic or environmental, or both.

Gwen's admission into hospital threw the O'Meara family into crisis. Robert, Peter, Helen and Annette moved in with Bob and Nell behind Bob's sporting goods and bicycle repair shop in Bay Street, Brighton, a couple of hundred metres down from North Brighton railway station.

As the days went by, Gwen's family were unsure whether Gwen would recover and be able to take up her role as a mother again. There were also doubts about whether she could return to work. Gwen would certainly not be able to cope on her own with the children for some time. Nell told other family members about Gwen's condition. During those first days after Gwen's admission, it would have been difficult for Nell to feel optimistic that her daughter would ever fully recover.

Bob and Nell decided that whatever the outcome of Gwen's illness, they would provide a home for Gwen and her children with them. They did not want to foster out the children and leave Gwen in an institution. Other members of the O'Meara family were not in a position to help. Jack and Barbara already had four children with a fifth child on the way.

Brian was single and running a hotel. Anne was a nun. Peter was a single Army officer.

At the time, Robert was ten, Peter eight, Helen six and Annette, was about to turn four. Bob and Nell were about to become parents of a second family in their late 50s. It would be an enormous challenge for them to take in four young children, who were each trying to cope with the loss and misbehaviour of their father and now, the mental breakdown of their mother. Jack and Barbara once again offered to take Gwen's children for the Christmas school holidays.

By 13 December 1962, Gwen's patient notes recorded:

> [The patient] has improved very well. Still inclined to believe in her voices. Talks about her husband's conduct.[26]

The next day she was released for two days into Bob and Nell's care. Brian picked her up and returned her to Royal Park. By 19 December, Gwen wanted to go home and take care of her children. Her doctor agreed that she could spend Christmas with her parents. On Christmas Day she spoke with her children, who were with Barbara, Jack and their children on the farm, by telephone. This was the first contact they'd had since her admission to hospital four weeks earlier. Robert recalled,

> Uncle Jack, Auntie Barbara and their children did a wonderful job caring for us over that Christmas period in 1962. We kept busy exploring the farm and its environs—catching yabbies in the dams, riding bikes around the dry, dusty roads and hunting for rabbits, lizards and snakes with "Butch", a small but aggressive, speedy dog that chased rabbits into logs and down burrows.
> Many a blue and red meat ant paid the supreme price under the slap of a well-aimed thong. Car trips were a real treat— thundering along the red earth roads singing songs, playing Spotto, or on Sundays, reciting the Rosary as we drove to Mass in Donald, breaking all records for the number of kids crammed into a station wagon.
> Speaking with Mum on the telephone on Christmas Day was

a real shock. I think I was in denial. I had already imagined the worst and had developed the self-pity of an orphan. No one had spoken about Mum for several weeks. I thought she was probably not coming back like my father. Her voice was tentative, like a child's. I remember feeling a huge surge of love for her. I probably mumbled something stupid over the phone. My sense of relief combined with a feeling of dread. I wondered if Mum would turn out to be crazy for the rest of her life. I had no one to talk to. Jack and Barbara were kind but they were not into counselling.

Butch (a rabbit hunter) being held by Martin Melican, Robert and Peter hold the rabbits while Damien Melican also smiles proudly

Four Breen kids with Martin, Bernard holding baby Nicholas, Lawrence and Damien Melican (front right)

On 25 January 1963 Gwen was discharged from Royal Park. Her patient record noted, 'Appears well. Rather stiff in manner and somewhat lacking in insight, but functioning well.'[27]

By this time Bob and Brian had been busy refurbishing several rooms in the rear of Bob's Bay Street sports store to accommodate Gwen and her four children. They'd also built on an extension containing a laundry, toilet and shower. Basic, but functional. For these efforts, Gwen and her children were forever indebted.

Peter remembers his mother's return:

> For me at this age [8 years], the time she had been gone seemed closer to eight months than to eight weeks. We were told someone special was coming but I looked for quite a while before I concluded that this was indeed my mother. The physical change was shocking. Her personality had been drained from her. Fortunately, as time went by, the life came back into her.

Gwen found that General Motors Holden had kept a job open for her in anticipation of her recovering from her breakdown over the Christmas-New Year period. She was paid for the weeks she had spent in hospital. On her return she was given a position in the typing pool—a significant demotion for someone who had been a senior manager's secretary. At 38 years of age

Gwen, aged by her stay in hospital, with her children, now living with Nell and Bob at 267 Bay Street North Brighton

she felt out of place among junior typists. Nevertheless, Gwen was very grateful to the enlightened personnel manager who had authorised her sick leave pay and gave her a job.

The year 1963 would be tough for all who lived at 267 Bay Street, Brighton. Bob and Nell set reasonable rules and rightly insisted on them being obeyed. This irritated the Breen children, especially Robert and Peter, who were used to being unsupervised and free to come and go as they pleased.

Meals were eaten together, hands were washed, and table manners were enforced and vulgar language forbidden. Gwen churned inside as Bob and Nell relentlessly criticised her children during meal times. Bob and Nell put themselves in the firing line as disciplinarians, insisting on appropriate standards of dress, hygiene, behaviour and language. Their perseverance saved Robert and Peter from becoming totally delinquent.

Bob was a big man who often sounded gruff and authoritative. However, his actions marked him as a man of great compassion. He was firm and fair with the children. Though sorely tried by their behaviour at times, aside from Robert, who received a well-deserved slap on one occasion, he never laid a hand in anger on his grandchildren. For this super-human restraint and patience, he earned their respect.

By 1964 Bob O'Meara had become the father figure, cousin Kathleen Melican, Helen, Peter and Robert Breen with camping and fishing gear

Nell was a different sort of disciplinarian. She brought a great deal of personal emotion into her actions when she disapproved of the children's behaviour. Helen, who could be quite stubborn, several times felt the sting of a slap, or the handle of a brush, or feather duster. Watching the consequences of Helen's defiance, Annette withdrew into herself and became a quiet, gentle and obedient person.

Gwen knew that Bob and Nell were doing what they thought was right. She also realised that they and Brian had worked hard and had paid out a significant amount of money to give her family satisfactory accommodation. She was grateful for the help she was receiving, but at the same time she resented losing control of her children and, from her perspective, being treated like a fifth child.

Fortunately, the living area behind the shop at Bay Street comprised two storeys. Bob and Nell lived upstairs with Helen and Annette sharing a bedroom. Gwen and the boys lived downstairs, which allowed for some privacy and physical separation; Gwen had still managed to hang onto the house at Regent Street, but struggled to pay off the mortgage. This was her only asset apart from an old Standard Ten sedan. Owning the house gave her some hope of moving out with the children once she was feeling better and more confident.

She put the house in the hands of an Elsternwick real estate agent so that it could be rented out. This way she could keep paying off her mortgage as well as paying Bob and Nell board. Over the next 12 months three groups of tenants lived at the house. The first couple were evicted after two destructive months. The second tenants were a couple whose marriage was breaking up. Gwen sympathised with their situation and allowed them to stay on, despite their payments falling into arrears. They left suddenly without paying six month's rent. The third couple absconded without paying any rent after damaging the property.

This series of events ruined Gwen financially and left her well behind in her mortgage repayments. The front of the house needed to be re-blocked, and because of the damage caused by the last tenants, surface repairs were required and the house needed repainting. Deeply depressed, Gwen handed the keys of the house to her solicitor and the Commonwealth Bank repossessed her home.

Meanwhile, the O'Meara family had their third wedding to celebrate. After several successful years in the Army, Peter, married Beverly McBride on 13 December 1963 at Toowong in Brisbane. Peter and Beverly became the 'glamour couple' of the family. Beverly had been the chaperon of the Miss Australia competition and was socially a vivacious and outgoing hostess with a wide network of friends. Peter, who was a handsome 30 year old Artillery Corps Major who had been decorated in Malaya for bravery, and Beverly were an attractive high achieving and well-connected couple. All of Gwen's children idolised their exciting, fun loving uncle and new auntie.

After a year in the typing pool, Gwen was again promoted as a secretary to a senior manager. Unfortunately this promotion turned out to be a disaster for Gwen. It was well known that her new boss treated his subordinates poorly, but they gave Gwen the chance to work for him because it was thought that he wouldn't treat an older, more competent secretary as badly.

This did not prove to be the case. He was pedantic, impatient and verbally abusive towards Gwen. On 24 July, 1964 she was admitted to Royal Park Psychiatric Hospital again. Her patient notes dated 27 July read, 'I had been upset with one of the bosses at work. I felt he was a twerp.'[28] The notes also stated, 'Says she hears the voice of God saying he is trying to save the world. Also hears other voices. Bursts into inappropriate laughter. Focus on saving Russia.'[29]

This breakdown was not as serious as the one the year before. However, it showed that Gwen was now vulnerable to breakdowns if there was any additional stress in her life. This time she spent three weeks in hospital. Annette, aged eight years, remembers visiting Gwen and coming away shocked and confused:

This was my mother, but the physical resemblance was the only indication of this fact. Mum was like a zombie. She walked like a robot, stared vacantly into space and when she spoke she sounded like a stranger. The people at Royal Park scared me. They were 'crazy'. Somehow I never thought of Mum as being in the same condition. The other people belonged there, Mum didn't. Only now as an adult, do I realize that each and every one of those patients was a mother, father, son or daughter of someone who loved them and was just as upset as I was.

The situation which had led to Gwen's second breakdown had left ill-feeling among managers and female clerical staff of General Motors Holden. In the climate of distrust, it was decided that on her return, Gwen could work on the factory floor where her duties would be repetitive and stress free. But Gwen knew she was better than that. She refused to take a menial job and left.

Once again she was unemployed and looking for work as a secretary. Many times she was knocked back after getting onto short lists and being interviewed. The uncertain mental state deterred employers. Finally, after lowering her expectations, she secured a job processing invoices at Cerebos Food Products in Clayton. In the early weeks at Cerebos, Gwen met and befriended Jan Pink, who wrote in 1995:

> It was 1964-65 that I met Gwen. What struck me was that her face seemed to be fresh and smiling. Gwen's manner, I recall, was open and pleasant, appearing calm and serene, even when confronted with the various complex codes for the food products and cumbersome invoice forms. ... During the years when we exchanged visits, Gwen would bring sweets for my two children.
>
> ... For the past 11 years, my life has been subjected to (much) sadness. ... Indeed, my mental health[sic] truly wondered how I would cope with even the next hours. ... Call it coincidence, mental telepathy, or whatever you may, but I have been puzzled that an unexpected phone call would occur or a short note arrive in the mail on a day when I had been in need of support. To hear Gwen's voice or read, 'I was just thinking about you

and thought, I must contact Jan', has lifted my spirits on these occasions. (Despite) communication for some years being confined to Christmas, how can one explain these surprise moments? ... I thank Gwen for her ongoing friendship. The strength I have seen in her, I have tried to embrace and consequently have coped with many of life's difficulties. I congratulate her on her life.[30]

Jan was one of the first women to draw strength and inspiration from Gwen's determination to rebuild her own life in the face of adversity. A great compassion had emerged in Gwen from the tragedies of the previous four years. She began reaching out to give comfort to emotionally wounded women like herself, and in turn, these women began reaching out to comfort her.

The 'Supporting Mothers' Years 1966-1970

In January 1966 Gwen turned 41. Her four children were at school and doing well. Gwen was still working, despite having to take strong medication to sleep at night, which made her nauseous and gave her headaches every day. Others in this situation might have slowed down and concentrated on not doing anything too stressful. Not Gwen. On! On!

A meeting at Prahran Town Hall in 1966 propelled her into what was to become her most important lifelong ministry and the next season of her life. Mary Spittall who was at that meeting recalled that Gwen had responded to a newspaper advertisement:

> ... concerning the proposed formation of an organisation for mothers who were bringing up their children alone. Gwen and I found ourselves together at the back of the hall and started to share our thoughts and ideas. We discovered that we had much in common and became 'friends with a mission'. I have remained so ever since. ... Gwen and I have each experienced many personal traumas since that 1966 meeting. I have never failed to admire the way Gwen has always come up smiling and closer in her walk with her family and the Lord. My life is much richer for having known Gwen Breen.[31]

Gwen and Mary had attended the inaugural meeting of what was to become known as the Supporting Mothers Association (SMA). The SMA had been founded in South Australia and it was planned to set up a similar organisation in Victoria. This meeting had been called by Reverend Frank Hartley, a Methodist Minister who was associated with the Labor Party, the trade union movement and pacifists. Frank Hartley was a controversial character who also agitated against Australia's involvement in the Vietnam War. Gwen believes her Granny May would have been proud of her involvement with Frank Hartley. She recalled later:

> I am a champion of deserted wives. I have worked with and shared with them since 1966. I got to know Frank Hartley when he backed the SMA. He is another of the men in my life whom I loved dearly. He had the guts to fight for a very unpopular cause at the time. I had a bit of trouble with my family because when my mother was having lunch she overheard two women talking and saying, "that Frank Hartley is a Communist". I never heard him speak of his other involvements until just before he died.
>
> He was so excited that the Catholic Church was allowing him to speak about the Peace Movement. Before then he had been banned. ... Whilst in New Guinea during World War 11 he made a vow that when he returned he would fight for peace having seen the devastation of war.

Marie Spittal and Gwen, close friends in support of
'deserted wifes' circa 1968.

Frank Hartley was known as 'The Pink Parson' and travelled to Russia frequently during the years Gwen knew him. He was a friend of Russia, social democracy, the working classes and the disadvantaged, but was no friend of Communism as a totalitarian form of government. The paradox of his commitment to Russia and Christianity was evidenced by Gwen when she attended his 60th birthday party. There she met the editor of the Russian national newspaper *Tass*, as well as most of the hierarchy of the Australian Methodist Church.

In the late 1960s, amidst the controversy over Australia's involvement in the Vietnam War and the rise of the strongly anti-communist, Catholic-based Democratic Labor Party, Frank Hartley was widely thought to be a 'fellow traveller' for the Communist Party. He had a strong social conscience. He passionately believed that the government and the churches were not providing sufficient support to women who were bringing up their children without the help of their husbands. This was controversial at the time because the Catholic Church strongly supported the traditional family as the environment for bringing up children. Non-traditional family arrangements were either ignored, or disapproved of as part of a general argument the Church was making against divorce.

The hurt and grief among many Catholic women who were abandoned by their husbands and partners was compounded in the 1960s by the guilt that the Catholic Church indirectly encouraged. The counselling offered by Father Maurice, who Gwen saw within days after Keith left, was a case in point. Catholic women were left to feel guilty and ashamed about the break down of their marriages because of the teachings of the Church.

Gwen took up the cause of 'deserted wives' as her personal crusade. This was to be her therapy and salvation from grief and depression, and also a means of exploring her own feelings and the meaning for her life. In turning outwards to others, she was supporting women who had been hurt and were grieving. In turn, their company and shared circumstances supported her as she sought some peace of mind about all that had happened to her as she struggled to bring up four children.

The most striking aspect of Gwen's devotion to the women whom she called 'her deserted wives' was the one-to-one efforts she made to provide them with comfort. She developed countless supportive friendships and continually followed up to make sure things were going all right in their lives. No matter what was happening in her life, Gwen always responded to other solo mothers in a positive, caring way. She wanted to show that there was kindness in the world and she encouraged optimism and independence. Above all, she told these women to pick themselves up, recognise their worth and take charge of their lives.

One of those whom Gwen helped, Thea Smith, wrote later in 1995:

> Over the years Gwen never forgets to ring and say something nice and always at the right time. ... Going through tough times emotionally, Gwen was there on the phone or at the door giving me encouragement and offering to say a prayer for me.

Marie Stuckey also recalled in 1995:

> I call Gwen Breen 'my true friend'. ... She made me realise that no matter what hardships one person experiences, it is important to get on with life. She helped me realise I needed faith in myself. ... If I have a special need I know that I can call her anytime. ... Gwen never expects anything back from me and I know she prays for me in a personal way. ... Gwen is a person who does many things which help many people, but especially women like myself who have had to cope on their own.

Gwen's personal counselling and emotional support was not the only service she provided to her 'deserted wives'. She combined her secretarial skills, her boundless energy and her love of helping people to become the organiser of many SMA activities. She organised an annual Mass at St Patrick's Cathedral, retreats, birthday parties and the annual Christmas party at the Central Methodist Mission, as well as outings to attend concerts in the city gardens and to the Melbourne Zoo. One mother recalled:

I remember so many little things [about Gwen]—like the pretty, bright dress she wore when we went to the Zoo. It was so colourful and it reminded me of butterflies. She glowed that day, as she often does.

Joan Ingle wrote to Gwen later.

My first memory is of the 1969 retreat. We walked down from the station to the Star of the Sea convent, and on turning the corner, to see you waiting at the gate to welcome us. Jane, the baby, was 18 months old and Norman, my eldest, was nine years old. ... Thank you for all the help and confidence you and SMA gave me and each of my six children. They each made the discovery that they were not freaks. There are many children out in the world without a father. They actually met some of them.

'Gwen having fun at at Supporting Mother's Association events circa late 1960s

Gwen went on to organise retreats for the deserted wives of the SMA each year for 21years. This remarkable service to others was conducted while maintaining a day job and managing four children. While Nell, Gwen's mother had no affinity with Gwen's ministry and worried, as did other members of her family, that her mania for service was partly fuelled by her mental illness, she and Bob gave Gwen and her children a home as well as a solid household routine to keep them grounded and secure. A second order effect of Gwen's ministry to other solo mothers and their children was the growing independence of her two boys, Robert and Peter.

In a similar manner to their time at the Regent Street, Elsternwick, the boys spent most of their spare time out and about at friends places or on the streets and public places.

Both boys were devoted supporters of the Melbourne Australian Rules football team, the Demons. Each year from the early 1960s they took out season memberships for entry to every home and way game and, dressed in Melbourne football jumpers and carrying red and blue 'floggers' [bunches of crepe paper streamers attached to sticks] attended every game. In those years they travelled by themselves to games each Saturday around the Melbourne metropolitan area.

Robert would continue his devotion to the Australian football game, while Peter lost interest in attending games and in hanging out with his older brother who wanted him to come out for 'kick-to-kick'. The brothers who had fought constantly during the unsettled years when Gwen and Keith were exiting from their marriage grew apart. For their part, Helen and Annette became closer and closer as sisters, isolated together upstairs from their mother and brothers who lives downstairs, and depending on each other for companionship and emotional support.

While Robert and Peter tested the boundaries of their freedom from their home and led separate lives from each other and their mother and her parents, neither chose a life of crime, arguably an option given the presence of criminals, like Nell's uncles, in the family tree. Though the permissive 1960s encouraged drug use, individual freedom, 'flower power' and promiscuity, Gwen's sons did not use their freedoms for mischief or destructive gratification. Unfortunately, each did inherit a fondness for alcohol, tobacco and vulgarity. Following the example of some older male relatives, as was common practice in the 'blokey' Australian culture of the 1960s, both boys smoked and drank before legal age.

One of the paradoxes of the choices the boys made during their adolescent years was their devotion to their mother but rejection of her religion, values and attitudes to alcohol and chaste, almost prudish, attitudes

Gwen with friends and Father Gerard Dowling, famous Melbourne radio priest offering family counseling on air circa 1997.

to the opposite sex. Gwen had not introduced men into the lives of her children, eschewed mixed social gatherings and, though she had a serious tobacco addiction, did not drink alcohol. She encouraged her sons to respect females and behave responsibly. Neither son took this advice and drank heavily when given the opportunity and sought the company of easy-going girls enthusiastically. Activities that came to Nell's notice and, despite her stern lectures about 'town bikes', Robert and Peter joined many their peers in this hedonistic pursuit.

While failing to convince them to follow a life of moral rectitude, Gwen made one fundamental and important contribution to her sons' development. Both boys would have felt great shame had they not passed their exams each year and completed their secondary education. Failing their mother, who often said, 'Get your Matriculation and you will have the world at your feet', was not an option. Both understood and loved Gwen for her unconditional love and courage in meeting the challenges of mental illness. Neither wanted to contribute to her worries and stresses in her life by failing at school. They idealised their mother as a saintly person whose respect for them was important. They followed her focus on getting a good education

Gwen with teenage Annette circa late 1960s

while never really discussing their subject choices, vocational preferences or study routines. They became autonomous learners and planned their futures privately.

In 1968 Gwen began her long association with Majellan House, a Redemptorist Monastery in Brighton. She attended daily Mass at 7am until the late 1980s when she moved to Bayswater. The Congregation of the Most Holy Redeemer was founded in Southern Italy in 1732 by St Alphonsus Liguori. Awakened to a fuller life while visiting the Hospital of the Incurables, St Alphonsus abandoned a brilliant legal career to give himself completely to God and embrace the priesthood in Naples. His compassionate nature drew

Gwen and her parents in the 1960s

him to devote himself especially to those who were untouched by ordinary pastoral care. His experience with them led him to found the Redemptorists. What was interesting about Alphonsus' approach was its personal quality— he connected personally with those who were marginalised on the one hand, and pleaded their cause on the other. The work of the Redemptorists in Australia began in 1882 and had built their first two monasteries in Waratah, near Newcastle, in 1887 and in Ballarat, Victoria, in 1988.

Redemptorist priests and brothers work through parish missions, preaching, retreats, adult education, teaching in universities, social justice work, counselling, accompaniment of Indigenous communities, chaplaincies, devotions to Our Lady of Perpetual Help, working with people on the margins of society and promoting the family through the Majellan magazine.

Gwen was an enthusiastic promoter of the *Majellan*, the family-oriented magazine published by the Redemptorists every three months. A frequent contributor to the *Majellan* was Father Max Barrett, with whom Gwen struck up a lifelong friendship. Max was her special confidant and counsellor. He was the first priest to pronounce her 'not guilty' for the breakdown of her marriage, to build up her self-esteem and remain interested in her life and aspirations. He epitomised the intention of the Roman Catholic Church to employ men who both accepted a life of poverty, chastity and obedience and lived a life of service. He was an ascetic who lived in single room accommodation all of his time within communities of Redemptorist priests and brothers. He was also an author of a number of books chronicling the history of the Redemptorists in Australia. In many ways, Gwen emulated Max Barrett's life of service, less his authorship, in a way that she thought constituted living a Christ-like life.

While working hard on behalf of the Supporting Mothers Association, Gwen kept her eye out for more satisfying employment. Processing invoices at Cerebos was not the sort of work Gwen was happy to do forever, and the long trip to and from Clayton took two hours out of each day. Eventually, fortune smiled on her.

Jim Whittem (then Assistant Area Commissioner of Administration for the Bayside Area Boy Scouts), wrote later:

> Ack Grant, Bayside Area Commissioner [for the Boy Scouts] wanted to set up a Bayside Area Office and Shop—a brand new idea in Victoria. Ack said, 'Can you come down to the shop and help me interview applicants for the position of Area Office Manager.
>
> Of course the title of the job we had advertised was not nearly as grand as that. You have guessed it—the first incumbent made it grand. And you know her name—Gwen Breen. Gwen was the only one I remember interviewing. She seemed to me to possess most of the attributes I was looking for, and as the years passed we discovered that she had a lot more. I think we got a bargain. I know my wife and I got a friend for life.
>
> Scout law says, 'A scout is a friend to all, and a brother to every other scout.' [By the way she did her job] Gwen modified it to read, 'and a mother to every other scout'—and that included the Area Commissioner and his entire staff—especially the Deputy Commissioners. Gwen worked hard, loved it, and made a minor fortune for the area shop. She donned the Movement's uniform herself. And found time to bring up her own kids, and helped with ours too.

The appointment to the position of Office Manager at the Bayside Area Scout Shop gave Gwen the means to combine her work with her volunteer activities for the SMA. All she needed was a telephone, a Gestetner printer, stationary and enough Gestetner 'skins', stamps and envelopes to send out hundreds of newsletters and other correspondence. She became an administrative dynamo for the Boy Scouts and the SMA in the south eastern suburbs of Melbourne.

Gwen was finally able to run her own show and be of service to many people. The Boy Scout movement and her SMA activities gave her an independent identity and a status outside the confines of her domestic circumstances. However, she did not like being dependent on her parents. She was grateful for Bob and Nell's charity, but there was tension.

The tension at Bay Street came partly from the challenge of bringing up Gwen's four children, and partly from the discontent Gwen felt about losing her independence as a mother. It upset her that she was forced to live with her parents because she could not provide a home for her children. She maintained her fierce loyalty to them, still like a lioness protecting her cubs. Gwen knew that her sons could be difficult, but gave them the benefit of the doubt. They appreciated their mother's loyalty, but Bob and Nell knew that it was sometimes misplaced.

Bob and Nell quite rightly felt that Robert and Peter needed strong direction during their teenage years. But Gwen resented the constant criticism about the way her boys behaved. The tension that resulted left Bob and Nell too critical of the children, and Gwen, too forgiving of them. Bob and Nell loved their grandchildren, but placed in the role as disciplinarians made it difficult for this message to come across as much as they would have liked.

From Robert and Peter's perspective, they lived in three worlds. Upstairs was their grandparent's world where it was wise not to put a foot wrong. Downstairs was their mother's world where there was little control, but unconditional love. And outside was the world of wonderful freedom, where they could do as they pleased.

The boys loved their mother and went through the normal phases of adolescence, but they also loved their freedom, spending as much time as possible in the outside world. Helen and Annette remained contented and secure in their mother's world, but were in conflict in their grandparent's world. Helen and Annette shared a bedroom upstairs near Bob and Nell but had quite different relationships with their grandparents. Helen wrote to Robert in April 1995:

> Gran ruled the roost with a good hard slap across my face usually or the wrong end of the feather duster or a brush. ... I was the rotten apple who was always picked on by her two brothers or Gran, and Annette always seemed to get off scot free even though at times she was at fault. I suppose I was destined to be the rebel who could do no right. I always wanted

> to get away from Bay Street and could not see why we couldn't.
> I was selfish and pig-headed but also felt alienated. I felt that
> you, and especially Peter, were embarrassed by me but used to
> be proud of Annette.

The competition for attention and differences in personality meant that Robert and Peter would protect each other against a common enemy but largely led separate lives. Both felt that being from what was known in those days as a 'broken home' left them on the margins of their school, Christian Brothers' College, St Kilda. Robert enjoyed being a member of the schools cadet unit and would rise to be the Senior Under Officer that would lead them on the unit on what was called the Passing Out Parade in 1969 and win the Returned and Services League Trophy for that year. Two years junior to Robert at school meant that Peter had his own friends, and spent less and less time with his brother, eventually losing interest in going to the VFL [now AFL] football with him. He joined the inaugural CBC St Kilda Rugby Union team that was started up and coached by Brother Frank McCarthy, who had studied in Britain and had come to admire the game as one that should be played at the 'better' schools.

For Robert, the comradeship of the army life attracted him and he applied for and won a scholarship to the Royal Military College of

Australia, Duntroon in 1967. The other attraction was that Duntroon had begun to offer a University undergraduate degree through the University of New South Wales. Gwen would never have been able to afford a University education for Robert. He was also attracted to the idea that he would no longer be a financial burden on Gwen or his grandparents by joining the Army

Robert Breen, attracted to the military, in his school cadet uniform in 1969

at 17 years of age. The Army allocated a few hundred dollars in Years 11 and 12 to assist Gwen with Robert's school expenses. This spurred him to apply himself diligently to school cadets. He learned much from the Australian Regular Army cadre Warrant Officer, Jack Sheather—the first of many men Robert would admire in the Army, probably honourable father figures and leaders that eased the painful memories of his own defective and treacherous father.

His father's treachery would surface again in 1967 when Keith sued Gwen for divorce under pressure from his partner, Jan, who wanted the security and status of marriage for the four children that Keith had fathered with her in the eight years since the birth of her first child, Garry, with the accompanying change to their illegitimate status before the law. Keith's suit was based having been separated from Gwen for eight years, an automatic means to achieve an annulment of their marriage under the legislation of the time—unless the suit was contested.

Gwen always wore her wedding ring and did not want the stigma of being a divorced woman, preferring to leave her status as 'married but separated'. She sought advice from the O'Meara family solicitor, Mr Sullivan. She didn't want a divorce because it would bring further shame on her in the eyes of the Catholic Church that characterised divorced women as both failures and sinners. Mr Sullivan, persuaded her to contest Keith's suit so that he would not have grounds to cease the paltry maintenance payments he was providing for the children. Assured by Mr Sullivan that divorce was now inevitable, he gave Gwen the choice to divorce Keith on her terms, or have him divorce her on his terms. Gwen directed Mr Sullivan to counter sue for divorce on the grounds of adultery and desertion. Gwen won the case easily and Keith was forced to make more equitable maintenance payments for Gwen's four children thereafter in exchange for legitimising four children he had fathered with Jan.

Throughout her marriage break-up and subsequent mental breakdowns, Gwen remained a devout Catholic. Her mental condition had deepened her faith in the Catholic Church and also focussed her distrust of Communism. Gwen read widely on the Catholic Church's opposition to Communism. She spoke frequently of her religion and her anti-communist feelings. Gwen joined the National Civic Council, headed at the time by the political activist, Bob Santamaria, and volunteered to do typing. She also became a supporter of the breakaway Democratic Labor Party—much to the irritation of Bob and Nell who remained strong Labor supporters after the 1954 Labor Party split.

Gwen's commitments to the Bayside Scout Shop, the SMA and the National Civic Council, as well as her four children increased the tempo of her life significantly. The stresses of Gwen's over-committed lifestyle once again began to affect her mental condition. In January 1969 she was admitted for a short time to the Malvern Psychiatric Clinic, after an episode of 'hearing the voices again'. Gwen's medication was increased temporarily, and she was able to return to work and pick up where she had left off. Gwen appeared to ignore this warning.

By this time, Gwen's boys were leading separate lives, involving themselves in the families of school friends and associating with other rebellious teenage boys. 1969 was a year of turmoil in the world and Australian society was divided over Australia's participation with the Americans in the Vietnam War. The 'rock and roll' culture of the Rolling Stones, Jimi Hendrix and Led Zeppelin encouraged individualism and anti-establishment behaviour. Robert and Peter joined many of their peers in trying to live out this lifestyle.

For Robert, 1969 was a year of great risk, but one that was saved by his determination not to let Gwen down. He recalled:

> I kept the wrong company, met the wrong girls and risked my Duntroon scholarship and future in the Army by staying out late at night drinking and smoking and not bothering with study. My pursuit of pleasure and exciting social times with 'bogan' mates resulted in a crisis as Matriculation examinations approached. In those days, everything depended on exams conducted in a two-week period at the end of the year. I locked

myself away in the caravan parked in the carport at the back of the shop that Grandfather used to take Peter and I to Stony Point years before for several weeks and 'crammed'. I am sure that the family must have thought that I was going mad. I smoked and studied frantically, only coming into the house for meals. I slept and studied in the caravan, memorising everything in an effort to make up for months of idleness. Fortunately, I was blessed with enough brains to get through.

In 1970 Robert began studies at the Royal Military College, Duntroon. The first of Gwen's children was out on their own. Robert recalled:

> I think Mum was happy for me to apply for a scholarship to Duntroon in 1967, even though it would mean that I would leave home at 17 years of age. I won a scholarship and was then obligated to pass matriculation at university entry level or give the scholarship money back to the Army. Not a bad incentive. However, my main incentive was Mum. She was there at midnight when the copies of the *Sun Herald* newspaper containing the matriculation results were thrown from the top floors of the *Sun Herald* building to hundreds of parents and children waiting below. I will never forget the day that she brought me a Harris Tweed sports jacket before I left for Duntroon by train in January 1970. We both felt very proud that I was to become an officer and a gentleman. She could not afford the jacket, but I got it anyway. No doubt she went without something to pay for it.
>
> I was happy to leave as soon as I could and not continue to be a financial burden on the family. I wanted to make Mum happy by starting a university degree course and becoming independent. Even though I would miss her, I would not miss life at Bay Street. I no longer wanted to feel dependent on the goodwill of Gran and Grandfather. I have never had to depend on the goodwill of anyone since.

In 1970 Robert completed his first year at Duntroon. He had found new brotherhood and thought his younger brother, Peter, would benefit from a visit to Duntroon to meet his new mates and attend the December graduation parade that was conducted on the second Tuesday of December each year. Peter might also benefit from the institution that had changed and matured Robert in a year. He hoped that Peter might also consider joining the Army and follow him to Duntroon and gain a University education that Gwen would never have been able to afford. Robert was also concerned that Peter was 'in with the wrong crowd' might be getting into trouble.

Peter, 15 years of age, and best friend, Ray Hoare, who also came from what was known in those days as a 'broken home', began hitch hiking from Melbourne to Canberra on the weekend before graduation but tired of their slow progress after being dropped off at Yass, about an hour's drive from Canberra. They stole a Holden Premier, a powerful car for its time, to complete their journey. They crashed it further up the road and the police drove both boys back to the Yass Police Station, neither Peter or Ray had a driver's licence.

Robert received the news from Gwen that Peter and Ray would not be attending the graduation parade due to this mishap. He returned to his rehearsal commitments for graduation after being assured that Brian, Gwen's brother was driving from Kyneton in Victoria to speak with police. Remarkably, Brian was able to negotiate for Peter and Ray to be released and accompany him back to Victoria. Subsequently, Brian managed the consequences of this misadventure, no offences were recorded and it was never spoken about again.

By this time, Brian had married Shirley on 24 November 1965 and became the step father to two daughters from her first marriage. In 1970 Brian operated a milk run in Kyneton, in central Victoria, and coached the local Kyneton Australian Rules football team. Brian was a generous, hard-working family man with a passion for football and a great contributor any football club he coached. Like many of Australian men of this era he smoked (Alpine menthol) and enjoyed a cold beer on a warm day—or on a cold day for that matter. He and Shirley were to have two more children, Veronica and Matthew and move to Ballarat later in the 1970s where Brian became an Enquiry Agent [private investigator], an Officer of the Court delivering legal papers and a repossession agent. A big man used to the rough and tumble of Australian Rules football, he was physically and mentally suited to the face-to-face confrontations that came with investigating the conduct of others, serving legal orders and repossessing cars and other items when people had not met their repayment obligations.

In December 1970 Robert visited Brian at Kyneton when on his first leave from Duntroon. He thanked Brian for what he had done for Peter. He also wanted to see him about buying his first car. A group of his Duntroon mates were going on a surfing holiday to Queensland and he wanted to join them driving his own car. Though only 17 years old, he had obtained an ACT licence a few weeks before. Brian suggested Robert buy a Ford utility that had been Brian's first milk delivery vehicle for a nominal price of $300 that Robert could pay in due course. The Ute had been in his garage for several months. After jump starting the car, Robert drove it to Melbourne and clashed with Bob O'Meara over his intention to drive it to Queensland. Bob felt that his grandson was too inexperienced a driver to be driving north in holiday traffic. He remonstrated with Brian for selling the car to his brash nephew, as well as with Robert for his foolish plan.

Peter O'Meara in Officer Cadet uniform with his mother Nell and auntie Val

Peter O'Meara as a young Artillery officer with his sister Anne

Robert was a stubborn, determined and over-confident teenager, wanting his freedom and asserting himself beyond his years after one year in the Army's tough officer training academy. He insisted on keeping the car and spent most of his meagre savings on a new battery and having the car repaired to make in roadworthy. He invited his only mate from school, another loner, Billy Frost, and younger brother, Peter, to accompany him on what he envisaged would be a great 'surfari' to the beaches of northern New South Wales and south east Queensland.

Another motive for this drive north was to visit Uncle Peter, an Army major posted to Canungra near Mount Tamborine in the hinterland of the Gold Coast in order to have Peter speak with young Peter and turn him away from delinquency. Both boys admired their Uncle Peter, who had in his teenage years been the 'black sheep' of the O'Meara family but had thrived in the Army after accepted for officer training at the newly-opened Officer Cadet School at Portsea on the Mornington Peninsula south of Melbourne. He had won an award for bravery in Malaya, married a vivacious and socially aware woman, fathered three girls, and risen to the rank of Major by the time Robert entered Duntroon. Though there was little contact while Robert and Peter were teenagers, to them Uncle Peter had become a distant hero because of his machismo, perceived glamourous lifestyle and rebel image in the family.

This journey north proved to be a stupid, dangerous boyhood adventure that included under-age drinking and driving, futile pursuit of female company and an unfortunate 'hit and run' crash into a petrol bowser. The Ute proved to be a mechanical disaster. Robert had to pay for expensive repairs for a 'blown gasket' and the repair of a gear box that leaked oil.

Quite stressed, Robert, Peter and Billy Frost arrived unannounced at Peter and his wife, Beverly's married quarter after a tough drive up Tamborine Mountain Road that was mostly unsurfaced. Peter and Beverly were finishing up a dinner party with two other couples. In the age before mobile phones, Robert had not thought to ring ahead. Peter and Beverly were 'in their cups' and found the sudden arrival of three visitors disconcerting as they hurried out their dinner guests.

An altercation between Uncle Peter and Robert followed, leading Beverly having to comfort Robert as he told her of his concerns over Peter and the challenges of his journey. Uncle Peter proved to be less sympathetic than Robert had hoped, and Robert returned to Melbourne, dropped off Billy and Peter, and returned to Canberra penniless to begin his second year at Duntroon in late January. He would never look to his Uncle Peter for help again.

The Adjutant at Duntroon soon told him that he had to get rid of the Ute if he could not get it registered in the ACT. Indeed, only cadets in their fourth year of studies were permitted to own cars. Robert drove the ute back to Kyneton the next weekend and left it outside Brian's house with a note stating that after spending nearly $1,000 on repairs during the disastrous trip north, a local ACT assessor had told him that the 'front end was buggered' and needed further major repairs. He wrote that he was not in a position to keep the car. The act of leaving the car and not speaking with Brian ended the close relationship Robert had with his older uncle. After this disastrous Christmas-New Year 1970-71 Robert disengaged from his family, more in shame and disappointment, than anger about anything, and became fully involved with the brotherhood at Duntroon and his new accepting Army family.

A Fateful Decade 1970-80

On November 30, 1970 Gwen told her psychiatrist that she'd suffered 'a turn' and was unable to do her job well. She felt depressed and was suffering from insomnia. Despite many assurances to her parents and other caring relatives and friends that she would slow down and decrease the demands she was placing on herself, Gwen continued her life at a frantic pace. She could not say 'No.' to anyone in need of her emotional support. Edna Fitzgerald recalls:

> To me Gwen is my guardian angel. In 1970/71 I was at my wits end. Housekeeping for an old gentleman, 24 hours a day, every day, every week, and I had my two children to send to school as well. I had about three hours off a week.
> One morning after the children went to school I was so down I took a tram to Caulfield and walked and walked until I came to the station and there on a billboard was a telephone number to ring if you were lonely and down. I rang the number and Gwen, my guardian angel, answered. Her voice and manner were so great and she helped me so much. Since then she has been my friend. Now I ring her and get all the help I need, so do many others. I love her.

Troubles with Robert and Peter over the Christmas New Year 1970/71 did not help Gwen's mental state. She was very busy at the Scout Shop at Gardenvale and was attending to the needs of several deserted wives, including

Edna Fitzgerald. Robert's clashes with her father, Bob, and brothers, Brian and Peter, as well as his insistence on being away for Christmas added to her stress. Her older son had turned his back on the family, though he assured her that he loved her, but would not return home on leave unless she needed him.

Six months later Gwen was again admitted to the Malvern Clinic Outpatients Department on 29 June 1971, suffering from hallucinations resulting from stress and her habit of ceasing to take her medication when she felt that things were going well in her life. This was to be a cycle in Gwen's life in which she would go through periods of high activity and high pressure, and then begin to feel that she could do without her medication. But once she was off her medication she became vulnerable to any sharp increase in stress caused by an event or other people's behaviour. Sometimes she sought medical help and returned to her medication. But if it was too late, she'd have a mental collapse. In June 1971, it was not too late. She recovered quickly after being returned to increased doses of medication temporarily in the following year she was not so lucky.

Her father Bob's retirement and a move from the familiar accommodation behind the shop at Bay Street to a new house at Cluden Street, East Brighton, were changes that Gwen and her daughters welcomed. Bob had survived two sudden heart attacks that warning him that it was time to change lifestyle. While deserving to spend his last season of his life with less responsibility, he chose to continue to support Gwen and her children. He bought 13 and 13a Cluden Street, East Brighton. This property was a single house that had been divided into two separate units. Each had two bedrooms, a small living room, a dining room, kitchen and bathroom, a toilet 'out back', and a long backyard separated by a fence.

In his will, Bob ensured that Gwen would always have a 'roof over her head' at 13a Cluden Street, for as long as she wanted to live there. He also made provisions that his estate, after Nell inherited and passed, would be divided equally among his grandchildren, not among his children. His older son, Brian, would be his executor.

Bob and Nell lived in 13 Cluden Street. By living next door, it was Bob's intention that he and Nell could continue to support Gwen and her children when needed, in return for Gwen's support as he and Nell entered their twilight years. The Cluden Street house was regarded among family members as the perfect solution for all concerned.

It was not long before Bob was there for Gwen again. He contacted her psychiatrist in early February 1972 to report that she had become excitable and unpredictable. She talked about grandiose schemes to save Russia and the world from Communism, and was difficult to control. Gwen had also told her solicitor of her plan to save Russia from Communism. He feared that she would come to harm unless she was sedated. On 17 February Gwen was admitted to Royal Park again after referral from the Malvern Clinic. This was a serious breakdown, caused by: 'stress of moving, ceasing her medication and death of Dr Wisewould, whom she idolised.'

Gwen was suffering from 'hallucinations and religious preoccupations, inappropriately laughing, hearing voices'. In a later interview, the Patient Notes quoted Bob as saying, 'Gwen walked stiffly, eyes were starry, [and she] 'is not with us.' Rather vacant. Crying at night. Upset by Dr Wisewould's death. Talks of Communist takeover. Had been sent home by the Scouts with a recommendation that she go on a holiday.'

After three weeks at Royal Park, Bayside Area staff welcomed her back and helped her to take over her old job again. This was a tremendous boost for Gwen's recovery. She feared that she would again be forced to take on menial work. She was determined to maintain her mental health and to meet her responsibilities after this set back. Jim Whittem, the Bayside Area Commissioner, and his wife Dorothy, were Gwen's strongest and most influential supporters.

Gwen did her best to maintain a more balanced lifestyle, but continued to be vulnerable to stressful situations. In May 1972 she suffered another episode of hearing voices. Married friends talking about their sex life during dinner in their home triggered this episode. Their conversation dredged up Gwen's feelings of shame and guilt associated with her being molested as a child and when Keith repeatedly criticised of her inability to respond adequately while they made love.

There was also the dilemma for Gwen to maintain her mental health and yet still be able to provide emotional support to other solo mothers. From her point of view, this ministry was a God-given mission in life. For years her family had been advising her to reduce her efforts to help others, as these activities were contributing to her chances of suffering further mental breakdowns. But just when Gwen realised that she should slow down and concentrate only on the essentials, two major family crises occurred which would test her resilience.

By 1973 Gwen was well settled into a busy, but manageable lifestyle at Cluden Street. Her boys were now settled and had promising Army careers. Robert had a steady girlfriend, Diane, and was due to graduate from Duntroon in December and Peter was in his second year there. The Army had recognised the latent potential of both boys and they had benefited greatly from military discipline and the Army code of conduct. The Army was also providing them with a university education, a financial impossibility for Gwen. Their departure after they had completed their Matriculation Certificates in 1969 and 1971 respectively had removed much of the tension between Gwen and her parents.

Before they left, both boys had been a law unto themselves for several years. However, despite occasional acts of delinquency, they had become strong achievers out of the love for their mother. Their greatest shame would have been to have become failures in Gwen's eyes. They also wanted to give her the opportunity to be proud of their achievements in front of some of the other family members who considered her sons ill-disciplined and likely to come to no good—a real possibility in 1969 and 1970. In the end, Robert and Peter had responded to a combination of Gwen's unconditional love and encouragement, Bob's manly and honourable example, Nell's discipline and vigilance and the Army's code of conduct.

Bob and Nell enjoyed a quiet life in retirement at Cluden Street, but there were continuing health issues for each of them. Gwen remained a respectful and dutiful daughter, though the years of tension at Bay Street had resulted in her not having a close and loving relationship with either of her parents. Considering Bob and Nell's good intentions, and the years of support they had provided, this was a great pity. Gwen was still uncomfortable with the implied child-parent relationship between them. She also found it difficult to express her genuine gratitude towards her parents for their support over the years, because she felt they were seeking a 'child-to-parent' gratitude, and not the gratitude expressed between adults who had a mutual respect for each other.

The relationship between Gwen and her parents was symbolised by the doorway that had been built into the common wall between the two units that made up the Cluden Street house. There was a lock on Bob and Nell's side but no lock was permitted on Gwen's side. Nell came and went as she pleased and was suspected of listening in to conversations between Gwen and the girls. In reality Gwen and her daughters had no privacy.

Nell's persistent advice to Gwen about Helen's and Annette's behaviour during their teenage years became a source of friction for all. She was concerned about Helen staying out late at night. Nell wanted Gwen to insist that Helen came home from dances and parties at the agreed time, but this was difficult for Gwen who took strong tranquillisers at night to suppress her schizophrenia.

Nell would enter Gwen's unit at night through the common doorway, and with a torch check that the girls were both in their beds. Though Nell may have had legitimate concerns, given that Helen had a strong, independent streak like her brothers, her actions only deepened Helen's resentment of her, and brought out Gwen's strong loyalty for her children in the face that anyone dared to suggest that they were up to no good

Tragic and unexpected events now intervened to test all relationships. The first crisis was Bob's death in 1972. Despite the distance that

Bob and Nell together in the 1960s

had developed between Gwen and her parents over the years, her father's death hit hard. Gwen accepted that it was now her responsibility to take care of Nell during her lonely years of widowhood.

The second crisis hit even harder and resulted in a massive emotional upheaval for both the Breen and O'Meara families. Helen, 16 years old, was pregnant to what Nell described as an 'unemployed boy'. Gwen decided to keep Helen's condition a secret for a while until she could work out what to do, though she'd told her psychiatrist. Helen was in love with the 19-year-old father of her unborn child and wanted to maintain a relationship with him. As well, Robert was about to graduate from Duntroon in December, and Gwen and Helen both decided that it would be better if he did not know of Helen's circumstances during this period of celebration. Helen recalled:

> Initially my intention was to never tell anyone about my pregnancy. The first adult I told was Sister Edwardian, a nun who had taught me at Star of the Sea. Between us we made up a plan for me to go to Queensland to live with my Uncle Peter and Aunt Bev [Peter was then a Major in the Army based at the Jungle Training Centre, Canungra, near the Gold Coast]. We were going to tell Mum that I was going there to do a 'Mothercraft' course. I planned to adopt the baby out and return to Melbourne.
> This plan fell through when I had an enormous fight with Gran [Nell] and had ended up in tears. When Mum came home from work she knew I had been crying and asked what was wrong.

My biggest fear was that I would be responsible for Mum having another nervous breakdown.

I didn't want to tell her. Eventually, I just broke down and told her. Needless to say, a few weeks later, after Robert's graduation, 'the shit hit the fan' and all the family got involved in our business.

Helen as a teenager in Nell's Cluden Street backyard

Helen with her siblings at Cluden Street East Brighton circa 1969

Helen, Gwen, Robert and Annette at Robert's Duntroon graduation December 1973

Robert Breen with future wife Diane Hardwick in 1973

Robert did not find out about Helen's situation until he returned to Melbourne from Canberra later in December where he and his girlfriend, Diane, planned to spend Christmas for the first time in some years. This would be Diane's first sustained contact with Robert's family. Nell made the serious mistake of ensuring that she was the first to tell Robert that Helen was pregnant to what she characterised as an 'undesirable young man'. Gwen was deeply hurt and angry that Nell was still interfering in her family affairs and usurping her role as a mother. From that day on, the Breen family cut Nell off from the more intimate details of their lives. She would only receive the good news from now on.

Nell wasn't the only member of the O'Meara family having a say about Helen's pregnancy. Barbara, Brian and Anne were all offering their advice. For Gwen this was *deja vu*. Once again, she was being assessed by her brother and sisters as inadequate. It was 'I told you so' time again. Gwen was angered by her mother's and siblings' interference in Helen's affairs. She was also angry about their hypocrisy. They were scandalised by Helen's pregnancy, yet a year before they had agreed to accept the pregnancy of another family member 'out of wedlock' because the father was a local boy from a well-known family.

At a hotel in the city, Brian, Robert and Peter Breen met to discuss options for responding to Helen's situation. They concluded that Helen was too young to be a full-time mother and it would be better if her relationship with the baby's father came to an end. They recognised that Helen could not be pushed. Robert suggested that she take time out to consider her options away from Melbourne.

After Robert spoke with the child's father and his family, it was agreed that Helen would move to Canberra and live with Robert's girlfriend, Diane, for a few months in her flat. Although Gwen had supported Robert's role as a negotiator during this period, she told her psychiatrist that she was upset by the family's decision to move Helen to Canberra. She needed to be left to run her life with some offers of assistance, rather than have all control removed by well-meaning, but interfering family members. Robert recalls:

> I was under a lot of pressure during the Christmas/New Year period of 1973/74. When I left for Duntroon in 1970 I put my family and my Melbourne friends behind me. I had become focussed on myself, my military career and my relationship with Diane—in that order, unfortunately. I was a self-made man, a survivor from the tough Duntroon training system and quite self-absorbed, self-confident and ambitious. I had not kept in touch with Helen or Annette during the previous four years.

At 21 years of age, Duntroon had trained me to be a self-reliant Infantry platoon commander, not a social worker. Shamefully, I treated Helen as a family problem, not as a person. I was more worried about the impact of Helen's situation on Mum rather than on Helen. In true Army style, I charged in to get the job done, get out and get on with my own life.

Before meeting with Helen's boyfriend I assessed that he would probably not mind if Helen and her baby disappeared out of his life. I proposed the Canberra plan and he quickly agreed. The unsaid agreement was, 'if I kept Helen away, he would not contact her.' I thought that moving Helen away from Mum and Gran (Nell) would help the situation at Cluden Street. Gran had made some serious mistakes in the way she handled Helen's situation. She and Helen had a deep dislike for each other. Mum was in the crossfire of these two very strong-willed, long time antagonists. Ultimately I wanted Helen to realise that she should adopt out the baby and return to Melbourne to start afresh. In January 1974 I thought the job was done. Helen went to Canberra to live with Diane, whom I was hopeful of marrying in due course, and I went to the 5th/7th Battalion at Holsworthy [an Army base on the south-west outskirts of Sydney].'

After several weeks in Canberra, Helen returned to Melbourne. She discovered that Robert was planning to talk to her about adopting out her baby. She wanted to be with her mother. These were confusing and emotional times for Helen but she knew that she could depend on Gwen to support her unconditionally. She was also determined to make the relationship with her baby's father work.

For the first six months of 1974 the controversy over Helen's pregnancy and her relationship with the baby's father, John, tore apart the O'Meara and Breen families. Gwen made it clear to her own children and to her mother, brothers and sisters that she did not want their help. The 'Canberra plan' had not worked. She and Helen would sort things out by themselves.

On 29 June 1974 Helen gave birth to a daughter, Melissa. She decided to keep her despite the advice of family members and the nursing nuns who attended to her at the hospital. Gwen was there in support. She was the only one who left Helen to decide for herself what she would do with her baby. She was giving Helen what her family had not given her. She was the only one who did not pass judgment. Helen wrote in a letter to Gwen later:

> All throughout my pregnancy with Melissa you were not judgmental, but were gently encouraging without any pressure being put on me either way [about Melissa's future], and I thank you for that. I know I could not have done it without you. We shared a very precious time with the birth of Melissa, your first grandchild, and, being the first to hold her, I feel that she bonded to you from that moment on. And to this day you have been the single most important influence on her besides myself and I am grateful for all the same encouragement you give to me throughout my life, you also give to her.

Gwen had also received support. She had sought the counsel of Isabella Kostas from the Catholic Family Welfare Bureau, who advised her that it was Helen's decision whether to adopt out or to keep Melissa. Gwen was grateful for this advice. It had helped her to adjust to her teenage daughter's pregnancy in the face of her family's attitude.

Once Helen had made her decision to keep her baby, Melissa was not short of loving, caring relatives. From Helen's perspective, however, the gushing acceptance of her baby after the rejection and censure she had endured during her pregnancy added to her anger. She remained distant from members of the O'Meara family, especially Nell.

Throughout this period Helen was trying to give the relationship between herself and Melissa's father, John, a chance. He visited Cluden Street once to take Helen out after Melissa was born. Nell did not approve. She ordered that John was not to visit the house again, and if the relationship continued, that Helen should leave Cluden Street. Helen reacted strongly. She moved out with John to a small flat in Brunswick. She wrote later:

> I had no intention of living with John or marrying him. It was only when Gran decided that I had to leave that we were pushed into living together. This was a month after Melissa was born.

Gwen was beside herself with anger and hurt that her daughter had been forced out of 13a Cluden Street, a home that had been provided for her and her family by her late father, Bob. The personal legacy of an honourable man. Brian, Barbara and Anne took Nell's side. Gwen supported Helen. The family rift now became a chasm. Helen left John some months later after enduring several beatings, and moved with Melissa into a small flat in Elwood.

On 16 December 1974 Robert married Diane at St Finbar's Church. Helen and Annette were Diane's bridesmaids. The wedding helped to reconcile the Breens and O'Mearas. Robert's Army family turned out and affirmed him and Diane for their wedding. He was forever grateful to Diane's mother, Mary, for paying for a reception at Ripponlea a prestigious mansion located in bushland behind the ABC studios near Elsternwick. Fellow officers who held their swords above the happy couple included Major Peter Cosgrove, Robert's former Adjutant and Rugby Union team mate at 5th/7th Battalion, with whom Robert would maintain a friendship over the coming years. Shamefully, Robert set the invitation limit to close family and excluded cousins so that he could invite more Army officers and their dates. He would always feel shame about this choice as the Melican cousins had been so kind to him and his brother and sisters over the years.

Robert with his bridal party, December 1974

By the beginning of 1975 Gwen was feeling good. In January that year she told a psychiatrist that she had experienced a great healing and was giving up smoking. She had stopped taking her medication and was reading a book entitled *Relief without Drugs*. Despite her previous record of breakdowns, this psychiatrist decided to take Gwen off her tablets. The result was predictable.

On 22 March 1975 Gwen was not feeling mentally well. She went to see her regular psychiatrist, Dr Arthur. His Patient Notes reveal Gwen saying that, 'the voices have come back again'. She was admitted to Royal Park the next day suffering from 'auditory hallucinations, repressed mood and pressure of speech, and feeling that people were putting thoughts in her head'. Helen and Gwen's long-time friend, Jean Bone, admitted her. At 17 years of age, Helen found this experience harrowing. This was the first time she had seen her mother in a psychotic state and also the first time she had observed patients at a psychiatric hospital. She wrote later:

> When I was 17 years old I had to admit Mum into Royal Park. My eyes were opened to what she had to endure there. She was so used to going there. She just accepted it as her lot in life. She was like a child reluctantly accepting that she had to return to boarding school. She knew the routine and where everything was. I felt very guilty about leaving her there. That experience changed my view on hospitalisation forever.
>
> At this time Aunty Anne decided to dump me with the blame for Mum's breakdowns. She said it was all my fault that Mum was sick. I did feel that I was to blame because I was always the troublesome one who could never do anything the right way. Anne's accusation reinforced my guilt. I carried that guilt for many years. I did forgive her eventually because I realised that she loved Mum and was in the same sort of pain I was in when Mum was locked away at Royal Park.

Gwen was discharged two weeks later after being stabilised on her medication. She assured Helen that it was the family's attitude to her pregnancy had caused the stress which led to her breakdown, not Helen's pregnancy itself. She bounced back, told her family to 'back off' and picked up where she left off.

Over the next two years, Gwen devoted her time to being the best mother she could be for Helen, and the best grandmother to Melissa. These were tough times for Helen who was suffering from tension headaches, struggling with relationship problems, and battling depression. Melissa was in day care while Helen worked. Gwen managed to drop Melissa off and pick her up before and after work at the Scout Shop. Grandmother and grand-daughter were establishing a very close relationship during these all important formative years.

The next two years brought further family stress on Gwen. Robert and Diane were struggling to have a family. Diane had suffered two miscarriages and it was uncertain whether she would be able to have children. Meanwhile, Helen had been involved in several turbulent relationships and was finding it extremely hard as a teenage mother. Nell was losing her eyesight, making her life difficult, and though Gwen continued to accept her responsibilities towards her mother, there was no reconciliation. Though Helen visited with Melissa often on weekends, Nell and her great grand-daughter did not meet or interact.

The year 1976 finished on a high note with Peter graduating from Duntroon and Annette completing her Matriculation successfully. Gwen took great pride in both events. Annette wrote in a letter to Gwen later:

> I believe that the person I am is solely because of you, Mum. The self-confidence I possess is due to the continual praise and encouragement you gave me as I was growing up. ... Your expectations of me were always high but not unrealistic. I believe I tried to live up to those expectations. I remember a favourite saying of yours was, 'As long as you do your best.' It doesn't seem that long ago that I was waiting for Matriculation results to come in the mail. Knowing that I had not really 'done my best', my big concern was that I would have let you down if I failed. Luckily for both of us I didn't.

In June 1977 Gwen admitted herself to the Malvern Psychiatric Clinic suffering from schizo-affective psychosis. The pressure of work and her other commitments had crushed her again. She had also taken herself off her medication several months before. This breakdown was worse than the one in 1975. She had a recurrence of voices and was in a grossly psychotic state—'crying, wailing, perplexed silence followed by howls of laughter'. Gwen remembers what triggered this breakdown:

> I remember very little of the admission. I came to a strange doctor's office [at the Malvern Clinic] 'wailing' as it says in the records. The wailing was from the hurt of my broken marriage. I was crying in the same way I had seen on a film on the television depicting the life of Henry VIII. His first wife was wailing from

Girlfriend Karen, Peter and Gwen at Peter's Duntroon graduation ball 1976

her boots at his rejection. I identified with her and cried in the same way. I remember the strange doctor saying, 'Mrs Breen, you are not listening to what I am saying.' That was the first indication I had that anyone else was in the room. I was completely 'off the air'.

Fortunately for Gwen, she was able to stay at the Malvern Clinic which was a more modern facility compared to Royal Park. She went through a period of deep depression after being heavily medicated, but recovered steadily. This time Robert was able to provide some support because he was living in Melbourne on an Army posting. Gwen's Patient Notes contained the following paragraph:

> Interview at request of son, Robert, who is an Army officer. He will be available to look after his mother as soon as she is discharged from here, as he is on holidays. Though quite friendly and co-operative, he admits that he has rather mixed feelings about psychiatry and would like to have his mother back home as soon as possible. ... Assured Robert that Electro Convulsive Therapy was at present not being considered.

Gwen once again vowed not to go off her medication and was discharged on June 20 into Robert's care.

Annette wrote later:

> One feeling I do remember having was that of anger. I couldn't understand why Mum couldn't stay on her tablets. At the onset of one of Mum's breakdowns I felt very angry. I was still living at home, so I was probably about 20 years old. Helen came over and I distinctly remember saying to her, 'I'm sick of Mum doing this. If she does it again, I am leaving. She can look after herself. I don't care anymore.'
>
> ... I don't believe Mum has a full understanding of the affect her breakdowns have on those who care about her. In a strange way,

she almost seems better off, as she remembers little about these episodes. I know she loves her children very much. So I can only presume she doesn't have that understanding, otherwise she would not go off her medication again and again.

Aside from a recurrence of hearing voices in December that year, Gwen stabilised and returned to work at the Bayside Scout Shop which had moved to new offices on the Nepean Highway in Moorabbin.

By now, the job that had been so important to her health and self-esteem 12 years before was proving to be too much for her. The Bayside Area had grown and there was more pressure on her to get things done for more people. Her great love of scouting was now putting pressure on her mental health.

Two happy family events were to occur in 1978. Diane was having a successful pregnancy under the care of Professor Bill Walters, a specialist gynaecologist and obstetrician with Monash University's teaching hospital at the Queen Victoria Hospital. She was due to give birth in mid-February.

Peter, now a Lieutenant with the Royal Australian Artillery based at the 8th/12th Medium Regiment at Holsworthy, became engaged to Rhonda, a nursing sister originally from Murrurundi in northern New South Wales. They planned a formal military wedding set for 5 May at the Duntroon Chapel in Canberra.

On 17 February, Diane gave birth to Benjamin by caesarean section. Robert, Diane and baby, Ben, left Melbourne a week later to live in Canberra. Robert was posted as a Captain to Russell Offices. Gwen attended her first grandson's christening at the Duntroon Chapel several weeks later and was in her glory as a grandmother for a second time.

Once again, however, Gwen had taken herself off her medication. Her timing was to rob her of what should have been one of the happiest days of her life, her son Peter's wedding. On 4 May, accompanied by Helen and Robert, she was admitted to the Malvern Clinic. Her patient file contained the following notes:

... work [at the Scout Shop] was too much and found herself giggling and chuckling through the phone or to her self. Had not been sleeping well. Not eating. Says that there were many emotional stresses recently—ANZAC Day and reunion with old friends, son's wedding, many functions to attend—felt over-active and was talking more. Dr Graeme Smith [Gwen's GP]: 'Patient has chronic schizophrenia, and has not taken medication for at least one month. She is not rational, is making unrealistic statements about religion and Communism. I consider her behaviour to be psychotic.' ... Reason for referral [under the Mental Health Act]: Discontinued Melleril two to three months ago. Over last two days was hearing God's voice (and that of world leaders) talking to her, and was making irrational statements about saving Russia. ... Had various emotional stresses two weeks preceding admission and became hyperactive. Her son is to be married in Canberra tomorrow. So this has no doubt increased her agitation.

A short time after Robert and Helen returned to Cluden Street, Gwen turned up in a taxi having absconded from the Malvern Clinic. She was still psychotic, but sufficiently coherent to know that she wanted to attend Peter's wedding. She was obviously in no condition to do so. Staff at the Malvern Clinic advised that they did not have a closed ward and recommended that she be admitted to Royal Park. Robert and Helen both hated Royal Park and had terrible memories of the patients in the closed ward, but they had no other option. Gwen needed to be sedated because she was becoming more and more agitated and uncontrollable. Late that evening Gwen was admitted to Royal Park. Robert negotiated for her not to be admitted to the closed ward. The staff knew she had never been violent and agreed to supervise her closely in another part of the hospital to ensure that she did not abscond again. Anne, Gwen's younger sister, offered to forego attending Peter's wedding to stay at Cluden Street just in case Gwen managed to leave Royal Park. The staff at Royal Park also had to have a relative to contact in Melbourne in case any emergency arose with Gwen. All the other Breens and O'Mearas would be in Canberra the next day at the wedding.

Gwen's four children at Peter's wedding to Rhonda McGrath in 1978

Gwen was missed at the wedding. Robert told Peter that Gwen was in Royal Park but did not tell any of the other guests. Everyone who knew what had happened did their best to ensure the day was as well celebrated as possible. For many guests Gwen's whereabouts was left unexplained. They were told that she had suddenly been taken ill and could not attend. It was very hard for Helen and Annette. They spent some time in the 'Ladies' crying and wondering whether their mother had finally put herself 'over the top' and would not recover from this latest break down.

Gwen was discharged from Royal Park a week later. This time she was determined to stay healthy. She resigned from her job with the Bayside Area Scouts while in hospital because of its stresses. She set her priorities on spending more time for herself and visiting her children. She was very angry with herself for stopping her medication and missing Peter and Rhonda's wedding. Her medical file recorded her as saying, 'I realise that I have to keep taking tablets for the rest of my life.'

Gwen with grandchildren Melissa, Ben and baby, Kelly, circa 1980

Grandma Years
1980-1995

In 1980 Gwen decided that she needed to retire from full-time work at 55 years of age. It was a remarkable achievement that she had been able to work for nearly 20 years after having her first major mental breakdown in 1962. Equally remarkable was the loyalty of the Bayside Scouts who employed her without question after episodes of illness. Gwen would be eternally grateful to Ted Whittem and his wife, Dorothy, for supporting her in employment and extending their compassionate friendship to her over many of those years, and would continue to be Gwen's friends for the coming years.

In that year Dr Arthur, Gwen's psychiatrist, wrote a telling summary of the nature and causes of her illness and the importance of her religious faith.

> (Gwen has had) schizo-affective psychotic episodes recurrent since 1962. ... It was likely that Gwen was predisposed to schizophrenia and that it was present at the time of her marriage. Breakdown and manifestation of schizophrenia was caused by desertion by her husband. Further episodes are likely, but hopefully neuroleptic medication will control possibilities of these episodes occurring.

> I think I should add that Mrs Breen's commitment to her Catholic faith has been a resource for her over the years of her psychiatric disability.

Dr Arthur's letter did not contain a full explanation of the contributing events to Gwen's illness, but it verified that Keith had delivered a severe psychological blow when he finally told Gwen about fathering a child with a teenage girl and then left her and their four young children to fend for themselves. Other events also contributed to the triggering of Gwen's schizophrenia. She feels she has never fully recovered from being sexually abused as a seven-year-old child. Nor can she dismiss the anguish caused by the priest with whom she sought counsel soon after Keith left, the local solicitor who sexually harassed her, the real estate agent whose negligence led to her financial ruin when she had to return the keys to her home to the bank, and the authoritarian, coercive boss who emotionally abused her at General Motors Holden.

Despite the mental illness she suffered as a consequence of the pressure of these events, Gwen continued to lead a life devoted to the service of her family, other 'deserted wives', the Catholic Church, especially Majellan House, the Boy Scout Movement and a number of charitable institutions. She still had plenty to offer. She divided her time between supporting Helen and six year old Melissa, doing a little clerical work for the National Civic Council, organising events for the the Catholic Solo Parents Organisation formerly the Supporting Mothers' Association (SMA), and attending Bayley House each week to help feed children suffering from Down's syndrome. She still attended Mass at Majellan House in Brighton every morning.

Three of Gwen's children were now living in or near Melbourne and more grandchildren had arrived since Melissa's arrival in 1974. Helen had formed a steady relationship with Don Dawson who worked for the New Zealand Insurance Company. Annette, also in a steady relationship, had completed her teacher training and was working for Gwen's sister, Anne, who was the Principal at the Sacred Heart Catholic Primary School in Altona.

In retirement Gwen renewed her quest for peace of mind and personal growth with added fervour. On 26 August 1980 she wrote to Dr Arthur:

> It was the hurt that got me and I just could not switch off. Yes, I had the cry, which helped me tremendously, but I was still thinking about my broken marriage and when the family spoke to me I just did not hear them. I felt that unless I took the tablets I would end up in hospital again as I could not get back to normal on my own, no matter how hard I tried. I do intend to stay on the tablets until after Helen's wedding as she has had enough unhappiness in her life and I don't want to add to it by being in hospital as I was when Peter got married. Thanks for listening.

Helen and Don were married in March 1981. Their marriage was a festive and healing event for the Breen and O'Meara families. The day was an outstanding success, attended by many relatives, and Gwen was in fine form. For Don it was the culmination of an important period in his life. He came into Helen's life as the supporting friend and companion she had longed for during the lonely years of single motherhood. In turn, she and Melissa created in Don's life the loving family that he had sought for many years.

He also gained a loving and supportive mother-in-law. Don recalls:

> When I first met Gwen I was a bit apprehensive as I was dating her daughter, Helen. But I was welcomed and accepted by her, much to my surprise. As time went on I learned that Gwen quite often put other people's needs before her own. She worked hard in the Catholic Solo Parents Organisation [formerly Supporting Mothers Association], collecting clothes to send to people less fortunate than herself. She sponsored (and still does) a family in the Philippines. She has always given freely, never expecting anything in return.

At the beginning of 1982, Annette formed a close relationship with Harry Syrros, an ambitious, self-confident professional pilot, who was working hard to 'clock up' sufficient flying hours so that he could get a job working for Qantas Airlines. Their relationship matured quickly. Annette found in Harry a sophisticated 'man of the world' who was supremely confident in his own abilities and opinions. This type of strong male continued Annette's predilection for self-made, self-assured men who appeared to represent the promise of security and protection. The risk was that the ambition and self-absorbed approach of self-made men did not necessarily come with loyalty.

When Annette moved out of Cluden Street to live with Harry, Gwen felt a deep loss. She was left to learn to live by herself and to care for Nell, who was blind and who needed physical and emotional support. Back to the future for Gwen from the 1940s. Despite her feelings of loss, however, Gwen remained unconditional in her support for Annette. Annette wrote to her later.

> I'd like to thank you for not being judgmental about any of my decisions I made as I moved into adulthood—only giving me continual love and support, even though I know you couldn't have agreed with every decision I made.

Gwen was the type of person who needed goals to aim for in life and enjoyed planning and organising for future events. Now that she had no work events to organise or coordinate, and had reduced her involvement with the National Civic Council, as well as Catholic Solo Parents [successor organisation to Supporting Mothers' Association], she set her sights on taking the world trip that had been interrupted in 1949 after meeting Keith.

She saved her money, carefully planned an itinerary, and convinced her close friend, Norma, to accompany her. A few months before their planned departure date, Norma was diagnosed with cancer. Norma encouraged Gwen to go ahead with the trip, promising her that she would take care of her 'from the other side'. She died soon after. Peter Breen recalls:

> It's more than I would do—set out on my own to travel around the world. I had been hearing about the world trip for ten years and must admit that I passed it off as a pipe dream. Despite the loss of her friend, Mum was determined. Now, I was worried for my mother but knew that she would soon make friends who would look out for her. Mum has the art of conversation and people soon recognise that they are talking to a truly genuine and big-hearted person.

Gwen and Melissa circa 1982

Rachael O'Meara, Peter Breen's wife Rhonda, Gwen, Melissa (holding fish)
and Jason McGrath–Sydney circa 1982

Robert and Diane with their two children Kelly and Ben Breen circa 1982
in Tallahassee, Florida

Nell O'Meara being visited by Peter and Rhonda Breen circa mid 1980s

Gwen left Australia in April 1982 for a three-month world tour at 58 years of age. Her first stop was the Philippines to visit Rolinda de Campo's family.

Originally Rolinda had been a pen friend whom Gwen had made contact with through the Majellan magazine. She was a teacher who worked with homeless 'street' children living in the derelict houses and rubbish tips of Manila. Gwen had been sending her donations for many years, accompanied by letters of encouragement, as well as religious cards and objects.

This was a fulfilling visit for Gwen. Rolinda's family welcomed her and a number of functions were held in Gwen's honour. Rolinda gave Gwen a suitcase full of Rosary beads made by the street children to distribute to friends when she returned to Australia. Rolinda wrote in 1995 for Gwen's 70th birthday:

> ... the sweetest of all my friends. Where can I find a friend like Gwen—loving, religious, understanding, caring, spirit filled, and a person for others—so Christ like ... loving God and serving His loved one too.

Gwen was able to stay for a few weeks on her way through the United States with her son Robert and his family who were living in Tallahassee, Florida. Robert, a newly-promoted Army major, had been posted there to complete a Master's degree in educational psychology and instructional

Gwen 75 years old with Rolinda de Campo (left) and Rolinda's daughter in Manila
during the second of her overseas trips

systems at Florida State University. By this time, he and his wife, Diane, were the proud parents of Ben, 4 years and Kelly 2 years of age. Gwen enjoyed her time with Robert and Diane and her grandchildren in Tallahassee but was to have her most interesting experiences in Russia. After many years fantasising about Russia and Communism, she found herself in trouble with a Russian customs officer who had noticed that she was wearing a crucifix on a chain around her neck. He called her over and asked if she believed in God. She answered, 'Yes'. He began roughly searching through her suitcase and discovered a picture of the Pope and a small crucifix given to her by her sister, Anne. Luckily, Gwen had left her suitcase full of Rolinda's rosary beads in London. He waved her through. Gwen went to Moscow and Leningrad, saw a performance of the Bolshoi Ballet, visited the Lenin Museum, saw the Kremlin by night, and walked around Red Square. She returned to Australia having assessed that the Russians were a lot happier than she thought they would be, and that they wore sensible clothing.

The overseas trip had helped to improve Gwen's self-confidence. Back home, she continued to work on various projects, which included a retreat and a special Mass for the Catholic Solo Parents. As she approached her 60th birthday she was often heard to say, 'These are the happiest days of my life.' There was also another grandchild—a son, Steven, born to Don and Helen in 1984. Helen wrote to Gwen later.

I remember the day Steven was born. I will never forget you telling me when Don came out of the delivery room and came down to you and Melissa and told you it was a boy after 17 hours of waiting. The tears still come to my eyes when I think of the way you described how you both hugged with joy and relief. And then seeing you and Melissa meeting Steven for the first time was so very special. You were also there for the [previous] miscarriages ... and were once again my Rock of Gibraltar.'

In 1985, after 12 years of widowhood, Nell died at the age of 81. She had been the matriarch and the remaining link to the preceding generation. Ill-health and blindness had diminished her capacity to enjoy her final years, but she had appreciated the tremendous support her family had given her during the difficult times, especially from her devoted grandson, Bernard, Barbara's oldest son. During those years as well, there had been some reconciliation between Gwen and her mother.

Nell O'Meara in later years with Gwen

Soon after Nell's death, Gwen's brother Peter, then 50, died tragically from a heart attack after the break down of his marriage and his ejection from his family home. At the time he was living at 13 Cluden Street next door to Gwen. His sister, Anne, found him lying in bed when she came to visit. He had died in his sleep the night before. Peter O'Meara had retired from the Army three years previously. Though he reached the rank of Major, he was not able to achieve his full potential because of an epilepsy attack in the early 1960s. He was medically downgraded and did not serve in Vietnam as did many of his peers. He served on and was appointed to some of the best postings available for the rank of Major in the Royal Australian Artillery. In 1974, after his service as the Second-In-Command of the Artillery School at North Head in Sydney ended abruptly after an altercation with the then Premier of NSW, Robert Askin, at a social function at the Manly Town Hall that became a media controversy, he requested a posting to Melbourne to settle down with his family and complete his military career.

Newspaper photo of Peter O'Meara in 1974

Peter did not adjust well to civilian life. He drank more heavily and had always been a heavy smoker. Gradually his health declined. Brian arranged for him to work with him for a time, but this did not improve his lifestyle. Eventually, he and his wife, Beverly, agreed that he should leave the family home. It was said by those who knew him that he had died of a broken heart. For his siblings, Gwen, Barbara, Brian and Anne, the death of their younger brother so soon after their mother's death was devastating. Befitting his devotion to a military career, he had a ceremonial military funeral at St Finbar's Church. Robert delivered the eulogy at Beverly's request and encouraged Peter's daughters,

Catherine, Jane and Rachel to remember the best of their father and take that memory forward as an inspiration in their lives.

In 1986 Helen and Don presented Gwen with her fifth grandchild, Anthony. Gwen's family was beginning to spread out across the nation. Annette and Harry had moved to Sydney after Harry had been accepted as a pilot with Qantas. Robert, Diane, Ben and Kelly moved to Singleton in the Hunter Valley in New South Wales on an Army posting; and Peter, no longer with the Army, was living with Rhonda in Frankston on the Mornington Peninsula where he worked for the Attorney General's Department.

Early in 1987 Helen fell pregnant again. She hoped for and received a baby girl, Cassandra. The family called her 'Cassie'. Peter and Rhonda, who were now living in Canberra, had their first son, David, in August. Gwen was a busy grandmother visiting her children and celebrating the births of their children.

In September 1987, Robert, now a Lieutenant Colonel posted in Sydney, drove with his family to join Helen and Don as they celebrated Cassie's arrival. These were happy times for Gwen. Her children were financially secure and had settled down with loving partners. Robert, Peter and Helen, were all blessed with children, and were proving to be successful parents. Annette and Harry were living together and there were plans for marriage and beginning a family.

Sadly, the coming Christmas was to be overwhelmed by tragedy. On the morning of 6 December, Melissa found her baby sister Cassie dead in her cot. Helen wrote to her mother later to thank her for the support she gave during the painful months that followed.

> When Cassie was born we knew this would be a special time to share with you because she was to be our last child. ... The first person I told that my precious daughter was dead was you, and even though it still hurts and I type this through my tears, I am so sorry for giving you that news over the phone. But I knew it was important for us to be together and there was no way that ambulance was leaving without my mother being there first. Throughout our grieving ... I will never be able to thank you

enough for all that you did for us. ... Through your example I
have been able to have enough courage to be able to, in my own
way, help some other grieving families.

Out of this tragedy, Gwen met Vic and Norma, who lived across the
road from her. They were to become her main supporters as she coped with
this catastrophic loss. Vic and Norma wrote later about how they became
involved with Gwen in the aftermath of Cassie's sudden death:

> Our valued association with Gwen ... began following the
> tragic death of Gwen's grand-daughter, Cassandra. ... As the
> weeks and months passed in that time of sorrow and suffering,
> Norma and I came to appreciate the selflessness and devotion
> of Gwen's life being given in loving service to her family. ...
> Gwen displayed a warm interest in people, including both
> family and friends; also a ready empathy toward all persons
> who are experiencing trouble of any kind. Gwen's infectious
> good humour, positive outlook, and cheerful demeanour have
> all helped us in our own family life, while her warm interest in
> our well-being has been a great comfort during the times when
> sorrow has entered our own lives.

Cassie's death brought to the surface a deeply embedded hurt Gwen had
been carrying with her for many years. Childhood wounds remain forever.
Helen wrote later:

> Mum had not let go of the pain she felt when her Grandmother
> killed herself until one day after Cassie had died. Mum and I
> were alone in my lounge room, talking about how we were
> feeling with our grief. She just started to cry, like a man
> does—right from her boots. I naturally thought it was to do
> with Cassie's death, but Mum started to sob and tried to tell
> me about Granny May and how Gran screamed at her on the
> phone. After this she was told never to tell anyone what had
> happened. Mum was still upset about Granny May not being
> given a proper funeral because of the religious implications.
> After this incident we contacted Lesley and Cynthia Bond [an
> Anglican clergyman and his wife] who helped Mum release her
> pain. They also arranged for a special service for Granny May
> to finally give her the farewell she deserved. I can't imagine the
> pain of keeping all that emotion locked up for so many years.

After Cassie's death Helen and Don grew closer and their love for their other children, Melissa, Steven and Tony, intensified. Helen turned to others who had lost children through Sudden Infant Death Syndrome (SIDS) and they turned to her. Like Gwen, Helen had found a caring ministry. She began year counselling and organising for the SIDS Foundation.

When Bernard Melican and his wife were told that their second son, William, would be born with spina bifida, Gwen was there to help and prepare them for the challenges ahead. She took their plight to heart and showered them with love and encouragement. She urged them to 'hang in there' and she brightened their days with letters, cards, flowers and gifts. She made continuous Novenas, dedicated Masses and phoned often to make sure they were okay.

Bernard always remembered having a special relationship with his 'Auntie Gwennie'. He recalled:

> To a young boy from the wheat plains, Melbourne was a mystery. ... I loved my January adventure at my Grandparents because everything was so new and exciting. Gwennie made me her constant companion during those holidays. I was invited along everywhere she went. We would head off in the Holden with bundles of clothing and boxes of food to deliver to the supporting mothers. All along the way she would chat to me—grown-up's talk—about things that were going on around us. The stories I loved the best were the ones that started with "Your mother probably wouldn't approve of me telling you this ..."
>
> Gwennie took me to her work at the Bayside Area Scout Headquarters and trusted me with really important tasks like going for the milk and ordering lunch. ... I remember sitting in awe at the Palais Theatre and absorbing the extravaganza of the Gang Show. Gwen had organised to take me and I loved every minute of it. At night after tea we would settle in front of Gwennie's television and she always found some money for a bag of lollies. ... I used to run all the way [to the milk bar] and bring back a bag bulging with enough milk bottles for all of us to munch on.

In August 1988, after a long courtship, Annette was married to Harry in Greece. Gwen was delighted. Annette aspired to be a mother and would start a family two years later. More grandchildren to love for Gwen. Her responsibilities and joys as a grandmother continued to increase over the following years. In August 1990 Peter and Rhonda were blessed with a second son, Alexander. Earlier that year Annette gave birth to a son, Athos, and their second son, Alexander, arrived in July 1991. Eager to keep in touch with her children and their families, Gwen began what were to become annual and then bi-annual trips to Canberra and Sydney, staying with Peter and Rhonda, Robert and Diane, and Annette and Harry in turn. She maintained close and frequent contact with Helen and Don, and their boys all year round. They built a home in the hills district of Melbourne near Fern Tree Gully and Gwen would move closer, initially in public housing at Bayswater and then Tecoma.

Gwen's role as a caring grandmother took on an international dimension in 1991. She responded to a call to provide support for those in need in Russia and began sending clothing and other items through a non-profit radio station known as 'Grandmothers and Grandchildren'.

The founder of that charity, Seraphima Lapteva, wrote about Gwen's support in 1995:

> The program's goal is to give help to children and elderly people, and to teach kindness and sympathy. We talk about children who are attentive and kind to old people. ... During our radio program we announce hundreds of names of boys and girls, big and small, and tell many heartfelt, touching stories about friendships between older and younger generations ... Children involved in the program receive letters of appreciation and parcels with clothes, toys and lollies.

> Mrs Gwen Breen, although she is far from Moscow, is a full participant in our work. Her parcels are carefully packed with this sign, 'To Grandmother Seraphima Lapteva—From Grandmother Gwen Breen.'... Across thousands of kilometres, across continents and oceans, spreads a thin, but strong chain of friendship. One end is at Bayswater and the other end is at Moscow.

Gwen during one of her regular visits to Canberra, with David Breen, Peter and Rhonda's first born

Peg Fitzgerald, her long-time friend and correspondent, also wrote about Gwen's boundless energy and service to others.

> Gwen's spirituality is very deep, but also very practical. I never ceased to be amazed at the way she kept her Supporting Mothers group going, despite very little encouragement. It must be 30 or so years now, and only God knows all the help and encouragement she has given to countless supporting mothers. Then there is her 'Clothes for Russia' initiative, and her on-going involvement in the Philippines, and her care and concern for the whole world. Above all, she must be the greatest grandmother in the world. My overwhelming inspiration from Gwen is the experience of her goodness, her kindness, her sense of fun and her thought for other first, then herself last. She has made a difference to my life, enriching it in so many ways.

Another long-time friend, Jean Bone, echoed these sentiments.

> Your life will always be full, because wherever you go someone will need you—a lame duck who wants a bit of care and help, or an organisation which wants a willing helper. I think you must have 48 hours in your day instead of twenty-four. Good on you Gwennie. I wish I were more like you.

Something that always filled Gwen with doubts was her effectiveness as a parent amidst this busy schedule of outreach to individuals and organisations. But these concerns were not supported by her children.

Helen:

> I don't want you to ever feel responsible for the fact that we didn't grow up with a father in our lives, because frankly, I think we were better off without him. I think you are a much healthier influence on our lives. The only thing I am sad about is that you had to endure so much pain from his leaving and you didn't have someone to look after you. Someone you could share the responsibilities of four children and all the decisions that brings. I think having my own children makes me realise how challenging parenting is and doing that on your own as you did would have been extremely difficult. You are the best mother anyone could ever want and don't you think otherwise.
>
> ... Over all the 37 years of my life you have been the singular most important person to me. I don't know how I would have turned out had it not been for the enormous encouragement, comfort and affirmation you always have given, not only to me but also to all my family. For that I am eternally grateful.

Annette:

> I don't feel in anyway deprived because I grew up without a father in my life. Perhaps this is partly because of Grandfather's presence, but I feel it is more due to the strength of the love that you gave me as I was growing up. When I think of you working full-time and then coming home to four children with all their various needs and wants, I can only marvel at how you coped. ... As a mother myself now, I hope that I am able to reflect some of the mothering skills that you have with my own children. I hope that I can give them the strength of love that you have given me.

Robert:

> The first 16 years of my life were shaped by your unconditional love, your fierce loyalty and your selflessness. It was not until I matured through life's experiences and took up the responsibilities of marriage and parenthood that I realised the significance of the role you played in my life. I also realised how courageous you have been to overcome the tragedies and setbacks fate served up to you. You never gave up fighting for your sanity, your peace of mind or your independence. Most importantly, you never gave up on your children.

> You should be very proud of your ministry to those who have suffered and are still suffering from marital breakdowns and mental illness. You have touched scores of lives and inspired them with the example of your own life. Never sell your success as a parent and a person short. I have been inspired and continue to be inspired by your courage, your determination, your compassion and your optimism.

Peter:

> My sisters and my brother have put it well. For me, mine and all the others you have touched, thanks is not enough. But thanks anyway, Mum.

Unbeknown to her children, Gwen was still seeking to be free of medication. She wrote later:

> I went to a GROW Annual Meeting and one of the Growers shared her withdrawal from prescribed drugs and sleeping tablets. She made it sound so easy. ... Judy and I went to a GROW workshop and one of the speakers spoke about how easy it is to give and how hard it is to accept. The message was that people are no more born to be mentally ill than they are born to be alcoholics, drug addicts, criminals, sexual deviants, slaves, ignorant or poor. These things are neither in our genes nor in our stars. People get that way through social influences and personal failure—that is, through learned habits of false thinking and disorganised living.
>
> In effect, the GROW message was that better thinking was a pathway to curing mental illness and doctors and medication were secondary and eventually unnecessary.

In September 1994 she stopped taking her medication. Many people managing mental illnesses yearn for the time when they will be free of medication that often comes with uncomfortable side-effects. Gwen was one of those. She had endured years of nausea and headaches from her daily doses of Melleril, another remarkable testament to her determination to work through adversity and lead a productive life. She started to attend meetings of the GROW organisation that promised to assist mentally-ill people to come off their medication. Gwen wrote later:

GROW says, 'Let go, let God', and that is what I am endeavouring to do. I avoided isolation as GROW says and decentralised another GROW piece of wisdom. I find Growers, as we call ourselves, are a caring and supportive bunch of people, we become like a family. On reflection I feel that it's not a case of who of us is unwell at times, it's just a matter that some people are more unwell than others.

In her 70th year in 1995, Gwen lived in a one-bedroom government flat in Tecoma in the Dandenong Mountains close to Helen and Don who had built a lovely home in an adjacent suburb in 1994. Her 70th Birthday party was a gathering of her surviving siblings, Barbara and Brian. Anne had died of cancer the year before. All of Gwen's children and grandchildren attended, with the exception of Peter, who had become estranged from Robert, Helen and Annette, over their decision to hold the party in Melbourne close to Gwen's friends and family and not at Peter's home in Canberra. Brian and Peter O'Meara's children were there with a strong contingent of Melican cousins.

This was a joyous occasion and one of great affirmation for Gwen. She received over 70 letters of tribute from relatives and friends. Helen thought it would be very positive for Gwen to receive these letters as tangible evidence of the way she had touched the lives of others, and how important she was to them. She was right.'

Barbara, Gwen and Brian at Gwen's 70th birthday party in 1995

Community service was still a major part of Gwen's life. She was an active parishioner at the local Catholic Church and was still organising retreats for the Catholic Solo Parents after forming a branch in Bayswater, Melbourne in 1992. Her new cause was the Australian Survivors of Child Sexual Abuse (ASCSA) that had been founded by Liz Mullinar (now called Blue Knot). She found a new understanding of the life-long impacts of child sexual abuse that comforted her. She used this understanding to comfort others in a local ASCA group that she founded in Tecoma.

Gwen kept in touch with an extensive network of people who have had their lives touched in some way by her, and who have touched her life. This ensured that she had one of the highest telephone bills in Melbourne. She regularly met with others fighting to manage schizophrenia and other mental illnesses.

The 'voices' returned in December. They were silenced after high doses of medication were prescribed. Gwen learned the hard way once again that she must continue to take her tablets. She wrote soon after:

> I had an episode in December 1994 and am quite aware that I will have to stay on medication for the rest of my life, which is hard to take as I've tried so hard. I followed the GROW program [trying to go off medication] and am now quite back on track.

Each of Gwen's children suffered during their early years, leaving deep childhood wounds caused by their father's emotional abuse, violence and abandonment. They survived, completed secondary education, partnered and began families of their own. By Gwen's 70th birthday they were emulating Gwen's devotion to duty and compassion for others. Each found the courage to beat the odds growing up without a father and with a mother burdened by mental illness. Each has an enduring commitment to their partners and their children, and to being responsible, contributing citizens in their communities.

In 1995 Robert, Peter, Helen and Annette were all married and settled in their own homes. All had careers and had accumulated between them three graduate and two post-graduate degrees. They had produced another generation of ten children—among them, Philip, who was born in February to Harry and Annette.

Another special event in Gwen's life was Melissa's 21st birthday celebrations at the end of June 1995. Melissa had grown up to be a self-reliant person with a sunny nature and an ambition to succeed in the hospitality industry. She lived independently and led a busy, productive life. She was the first of another generation of Gwen's family to stand on her own two feet and succeed in whatever she set out to do.

After her 70th Birthday Gwen wanted to pass on what her past 70 years had taught her. She wrote in 1995:

> When I was told I'd been diagnosed schizophrenic, I felt like someone who had been "kicked in the guts". I have been trying to have the label changed, with no success. It is very distressful. I carried that winded feeling around with me for quite a few years.
>
> I have also had the label 'manic depressive' [also known as bi-polar mood disorder] as a diagnosis for my illness. Manic components are activity, energy, sociability, cheerfulness, enthusiasm, optimism, drive, alertness and warmth. On the down side, the depressive components are, inactivity, dissatisfaction, lacking vitality, doubts, lacking confidence, tearful, despondent, over-anxious, insecure and indecisive.
>
> Thirty-five odd years ago I was diagnosed as 'chronic schizophrenic.' On my journey towards mental wellness I obtained some knowledge that I would like to share with you, with a view to helping those who are suffering from mental illness. I discovered I had to get in touch with my feelings.
>
> I learned that thoughts come before feelings, you can control your thoughts, and therefore you can control your feelings. My thoughts help me to get in touch with myself. They let me know what is going on in me. They alert me to the need to "depth" the feeling (if it feels good), or to arrest and re-direct the feeling (if it feels negative). I found thinking of a pleasant experience which made me feel good helped. This is called transmuting. Feelings are neither right nor wrong—just feelings. It is what

you do with those feelings that counts. Negative feelings feed on negative thoughts.

An exercise I found helpful was:

1   NAME—Recognise the feeling.

2   CLAIM—Own up to the feeling.

3   TAME—Control the feeling. This may entail sharing my trial with a trusted person.

4   AIM—To be content.

5   BLAME—Do not blame anyone else for our feelings.

I also learnt that we can only deal with extreme feelings in the following ways.

MAD—Anger. Forgive ourselves and all others is the key to controlling anger.

BAD—Depression. Eliminate negative thoughts. One thought being guilt—make sure it is not phoney guilt. If it is true guilt, then repent and be assured that God has forgiven you.

SAD—Grief. Grieving over the loss of any sort. Acceptance of loss is a step in the right direction.

GLAD—Contentment.

SCARED—Anxiety. Let go. Let God in.

HURT—I learned that hurt can turn into anger or depression. Before it does either, take some deep breaths to control the adrenalin and bring the blood pressure down, and restore the sanity of a right sense of proportion.

Forgiveness is an attitude. You do not have to feel warmly towards the forgiven person. Confidence is an attitude.

HEALING—I would like to share with you one of my healings. I have had others but I think this one will illustrate how important getting in touch with your feelings can be.

I was sexually molested at the age of seven years and when I shared this experience with a priest [Father Max Barrett], he said, 'Not guilty.' I thought to myself, 'Was I feeling guilty?' A few months later I found myself sobbing uncontrollably and I realised that I had been feeling guilty for all those years. I realised that I had harboured this negative phoney guilt feeling for over 40 years. Once I recognised the feeling, I could deal with it.

Negative feelings alert me to the need to take charge of my own life and not allow feelings to take charge of me. I took charge by breaking out of my 'stinking thinking.'

Getting in touch with our feelings and learning to accept them as part of our being can be painful and exhausting, but Oh so rewarding. We have choices. God has given us free will, therefore we should use it. One very important fact I learned was: I AM SPECIAL.

In 1995 Gwen summed up 'my present position' thus:

I am a Labor voter. I support the Aborigines and am a Republican. I continue to write letters when something I feel strongly about stirs me into action.

I have complete empathy with 'deserted wives' and the mentally ill.

I cry sometimes at God's goodness to me, I am indeed a lucky lady. As Mother Mary Mackillop says, 'Look back and see what the Good Lord has done for you.' I can certainly see God's hand in my life.

I try to maintain my sense of humour which is vital to staying afloat.

Robert wrote this book [first edition] with the firm belief that it will help others. I sincerely hope that it does that.

I am presently working on Confidence and Control which is part of the GROW program.

I would never have had as interesting or fulfilling life as I've had had I still been legally married to Keith.

The Twilight Years 1995-2012

Before and after her 70th Birthday in January 1995, family and friends affirmed and encouraged Gwen. She was settled in Tecoma in a one-bedroom flat within a public housing estate and enjoyed a busy life of community service to a number of organisations. First and foremost was St Thomas More's Parish in Terry Street, Belgrave. She maintained her faith and devotion to the Catholic Church there. Her interaction with the Parish priest was an important aspect of her faith and sense of well-being. This had been so when she attended Mass on a daily basis at Majellan House in Brighton. Priests supported Gwen and she supported them. She drew strength, purpose and commitment to the common good and the disadvantaged from inspirational priests. She felt that she belonged at St Thomas More's and was valued and respected there.

While the Roman Catholic Church was replete with idiosyncratic, elderly priests by the 1990s, St Thomas More was blessed with young priests from either minor priestly orders who wore sandals or priests recruited from ethnic minorities, such as the strongly Catholic Vietnamese community who had settled in Australia after the end of the Vietnam War, many arriving as infants on boats. She was blessed with a number of people who would drive her to Mass on Sunday's. Unable to drive anymore, daily Bible study had to replace her daily Mass routine. Marie Sheahan was her stalwart 'chauffeur' on Sundays. Faye Claxton, drove from Glen Waverly to help her with her shopping as her breathlessness increased and mobility decreased over time.

Gwen's circle of friends included members of the former Supporting Mothers Association, the Women's Action Alliance, the Ex-WRANS Association and Advocates for Survivors of Child Abuse (ASCA). Copying Christ's inclusiveness and the time he spent with society's marginalised people, Gwen supported several battlers whose circumstances challenged them. She convened an ASCA group in Tecoma in order to comfort those who had been sexually abused as children and were finding that childhood wounds remained open and disrupted their adult lives. One member of the ASCA group was Zavian, whom Gwen described as a hermaphrodite [intersexual or transgender person]. Gwen was the friend that Zavian needed as she battled with drug addiction, the impact of childhood sexual exploitation and ongoing relationship problems. Non-judgemental and positive, Gwen was available to answer Zavian's calls '24/7', often calming her when she was in crisis.

A Women's Action Alliance newsletter in 2001 described Gwen's life thus:

> Gwen Breen, a long term member as well as a [former] committee member of the WAA for several years, has had a very diverse life, joining the WRANS at 18 and serving for three years in the [Royal Australian Navy's] communications branch [enlisting on 8 February 1943 and honourably discharged on 28 February 1946, achieving the rank of Leading Tele printer Operator].[32]

> She then went on to nursing before marrying. Tragedy struck when her husband left her with four children under the age of six to bring up on her own. She was also stricken by schizophrenia.

> These experiences gave Gwen a great empathy for sick and disadvantaged people, and since she retired from paid work she has devoted herself to helping others. ... since she moved to the Hills, she works for the Boronia Baptists Centre for

Special Needs Children—giving respite care so that mothers could have a break. ... Gwen has spread her interests wide, from area Secretary of scouting, to Executive Committee Member of the ex-WRANS Association, to the Tecoma Group of Advocates for Survivors of Child Abuse. ... Gwen always gives total support and devotion to her children and grandchildren.

Emulating her Granny May's interest in promoting peace in the world, Gwen had joined her close friend from her childhood in Brighton, Peg Fitzgerald, many years before in volunteering for Pax Christi, an Australia-wide Christian Peace Movement that stood against militarism and the arms race. Central to its work were human rights, justice and 'integrity of creation' and fostering the spiritual and scriptural dimensions of peacemaking. Drawing on her Irish roots and a vision for a reconciled Australia well before reconciliation became a bi-partisan Australian Government endeavour, she told a Pax Christi conference in 1998 that the British flag in the corner of the Australian flag should be replaced with the Aboriginal flag.[33]

Gwen's children and grandchildren were a big part of her life in the late 1990s. Helen and Don, and their boys Steven and Tony lived in Tecoma a few minutes' drive away. She was a welcome guest for meals and family events. Helen was a book keeper and Don worked as a manager of worker's compensation claims. They had a lovely home in the bush in Tecoma where Gwen's 70th Birthday celebrations had been held. Melissa, in her early 20s, was working in Sydney. Robert and Diane were in Sydney in their own home at Kingsford near Randwick Barracks with son, Ben, and daughter, Kelly. The ABC program *The Home Show* had covered Robert and Diane's renovations in a weekly television series. Robert was a vocational education and training consultant, a Lieutenant Colonel in the Army Reserve and a military historian. He had a contract with Defence to work as an Operations Analyst for the Land Commander, who commanded ADF overseas operations from Victoria Barracks in Paddington. He had been deployed to Somalia, Rwanda, and southern Lebanon and in 1997 started to spend a few weeks every three months in Cape York training civilian peace monitors about to serve in Bougainville, Papua New Guinea's eastern-most island province, as well as advising Australian commanders on the Bougainville peacekeeping operation. Diane taught at St Andrew's Catholic primary school at Malabar. Annette and Harry lived in western Sydney in their own home and now had three boys, Athos, Alex and baby, Phillip. Harry was a second officer with Qantas Airlines and Annette was a primary school teacher. Peter and Rhonda were in Canberra in their own home in Weetangera. Peter worked for the Attorney General's department and Rhonda was a nursing sister at John James Private Hospital. They had two boys, David and Alex.

Gwen at Peter and Rhonda's home in Canberra with David (left and Alex (right) in 2003

Gwen's next health challenge occurred in 1997 and into 1998 when she was diagnosed with breast cancer. She received treatment and had a single mastectomy in 1997. This was a worrying time because Gwen's sister, Anne, had died in August 1994 after a long battle with cancer. Gwen and her family hoped that her treatment and surgery would result in a long remission and that the cancer might not return or manifest itself elsewhere in her body. With impressive resilience, Gwen rebounded from her surgery and radiation treatment and returned to her flat at Tecoma rather than seeking residence in a nursing home. In 1998 there was no sign of the cancer returning so she resumed travelling to see her family. She visited Robert and his family and Annette and her boys in Sydney during the year, as well as Peter and his family in Canberra for Christmas—a tradition of many years.

In 1998 Gwen featured in the *Whitehorse Post* promoting ASCA. She shared for the first time her own story publically, telling the newspaper:

> It [The sexual abuse] took away my childhood—I never remember being a child. I didn't tell anyone what happened until nearly 30 years ago and I'm 73 years old now. I kept it a secret because of family loyalty.[34]

Gwen with a friend circa 2001

The paper reported that, 'Gwen decided to set up a local branch of the ASCA in Tecoma in a bid to 'break the silence and help other survivors of child abuse speak out'.

On 30 January 1999 two weeks after her 74th birthday, Brian, Gwen's younger brother, died in Ballarat from a sudden heart attack aged 68 years. Brian had spent the years since an acrimonious divorce from Shirley living alone and not really taking care of himself. The funeral was held on 4 February at St Patrick's Cathedral. Brian was remembered at his funeral as a loving grandfather and caring family man. He was always kind and communicated

Brian O'Meara in later years

with a gentle mocking, playful humour characteristic of his Irish heritage. He had intervened several times in the lives of Gwen's children for their betterment. Peter never forgot Brian's mercy dash to get him out of the Yass police lock up in 1970. Annette appreciated him helping her buy her first car. Forgiving the 1970 Ute kerfuffle, Robert appreciated that Brian insisted that his prestigious big Ford LTD car be used to transport Diane and the bridesmaids to his wedding in 1974. Brian stood by in support of his family for his entire life and could be relied on to help if asked. The local police Criminal Investigation Branch and Ballarat Court Staff acknowledged Brian's work as Enquiry Agent at his funeral. His nephew, Bernard, delivered a moving eulogy to the O'Meara family's gentle giant. Brian was survived by his step daughter, Susan and grandson Beau, and other estranged step daughter, Cheryl. His daughter Veronica, and her two children, Alexandra and Zachary, and his son, Matthew. They would miss a loving father and grand-father.

The new century began with Gwen taking a trip at 75 years of age to Israel and Egypt in early 2000 to see the places where her father Bob had served and to visit shrines commemorating the important locations in the Bible. This trip was made difficult because her suitcase was lost by the airlines early in her trip and she had to endure the cold dressed only in slacks and a T-shirt. It was heartbreaking for family members to see photos of Gwen in a T-shirt with the other tour bus passengers rugged up in jackets and scarves. She had not thought to reach out to her children to send her money to pay for more clothes. Despite this inconvenience, she had a wonderful time and made several good friends along the way that she would correspond with for many years afterwards.

Keith Breen died in 2001 of Myeloma cancer of the blood. Gwen was 76 years of age but was still hurting over her broken marriage. She wrote at the time that 'a sudden anger welled up' when he died and she realised

Keith Breen as an older man, father of eight children with two women, still playing his saxophone

that the emotional impact of his desertion was lifelong. Helen attended
Keith's funeral and found that no mention was made in his eulogy of his
first marriage to Gwen and his first four children. His wife, Jan, had gone
on to have four children as well, none of whom knew that they had two half-
brothers and two half-sisters. Helen spoke to Gary, Keith's eldest son, who
confirmed that Keith had continued to be a violent, negligent father. Gary
had run away from home as teenager to get away from him. One of Gary's
brothers-in-law had given the eulogy because none of his children wished
to do so. Helen had to leave the church quickly as Jan spotted her talking to
Gary and giving him a copy of the first edition of this book. No contact was
made between Keith's two families groups of children after his funeral.

In 2002 Gwen faced another family disappointment when Robert's
marriage failed. Much to everyone's surprise he announced, after
returning from service as a United Nations volunteer in East Timor in
May 2002 that Diane had put down a deposit on an apartment in Sans
Souci and was moving out. This came as a shock. Robert had been in
daily contact with Diane by phone and did not suspect that the end of
his marriage was awaiting him when he returned to Sydney. Gwen and
Robert kept in contact and she comforted him after the initial shock and
along what became a painful journey.

A year later in 2003 the marriage of the second of Gwen's children
failed. Annette moved out to a rented house in Bowral while Harry
stayed at the home he had built on the sizeable parcel of land he hoped to
subdivide into allotments for aged care townhouses. The boys lived with
Annette and visited Harry when he was in Bowral once a week for dinner.
Harry was an attentive father is some ways and stumped up for each boy's
education at the nearby Oxley independent Anglican College and assisted
them financially in other ways.

There was some good news for Robert by this time. He had met and
become engaged to Nicola Crichton, a young woman 20 years his junior
who suffered from Bi-polar Mood Disorder. They had met at the Defence

Archives in Queanbeyan in late 2002. Nicola's parents, Bill and Dodie, and her sisters, Sarah and Eliza were delighted that an older man was taking care of Nicola and giving her the love, security and stability she needed to develop herself after almost ten years at home with her parents struggling with self-confidence and managing her illness. Having grown up with Gwen's illness, Robert thought that he had a reasonable chance of making this partnership work.

Gwen and Nicola 'hit it off' immediately as each told the other of their battles with mental illness. Gwen became an important role model for Nicola and loved her as another daughter. She took great delight in knowing that Robert had a new loving partner, telling him that Nicola was his intended companion for the next season of his life. Nicola, a talented artist who had to give up her studies for a degree in Fine Arts at ANU because of her illness, reciprocated Gwen's love and drew a wonderful portrait of Gwen (see back cover). Bob looked forward to providing Nicola a home with a studio in due course. For the time being, he and Nicola moved into a flat at Kirribilli in Sydney opposite Circular Quay and extended hospitality to family and friends, especially for the New Year's Eve fireworks display. Their engagement party in January 2004 was on a ferry sailing around Sydney Harbour. A wonderful start to a new relationship for Robert and Nicola's family and friends.

In 2005, Gwen turned 80 years of age and a big contingent of family and friends gathered at a function centre near Tecoma to celebrate this important 'four score' birthday. The Melicans were there and both families deepened their relationships. The only clouds on the horizon were Gwen's health issues. The breast cancer returned. She resumed treatment and had limp nodes removed to stop the cancer's spread. Fortunately, early detection and prompt treatment resulted in a second remission. Her breathlessness caused by her fragile heart valve worsened. She had a major operation to remove a gall stone that she described as 'as big as a duck's egg' and mobility was becoming a major limitation to independent living.

Nicola and Gwen in Canberra again for Christmas 2003

Gwen with Kelly and Ben, at Robert and Nicola's wedding in 2004

Gwen with Robert and Nicola at their wedding in 2004

In 2006 Helen's 50th Birthday was a very happy family occasion. It was held at her son, Steven's and his partner, Sally's, home in Tecoma. Melissa did most of the organising and provided resources for a great gathering of family and friends. Nicola, Robert's wife, gave Helen a lovely painting. She had been inspired to represent Helen and her children as blooming roses. In the same year, Robert and Nicola and Helen and Don visited Melissa, who was driving tourist buses at Uluru in the Northern Territory. Melissa did a wonderful job of organised events and experiences for her parents and her uncle and his wife at Uluru.

Later in 2006 Gwen knew that she had to go into care. Her mobility was diminishing with arthritis in her knees and she suffered from constant breathlessness. Her second struggle with breast cancer at 80 years of age had left her 'at risk' if she was not close to medical facilities. Sadly, she and Helen fell out over her choice of aged care facility in Melbourne. Gwen favoured a place some distance away from Tecoma that had been a convent and had daily Mass. She was not deterred by the prospect of communal bathroom and toilet arrangements rather than having ensuite facilities. None of Gwen's children wanted her to go into these substandard facilities, but Gwen was determined and had every right to select her own accommodation. Unfortunately, she had not thought through the implications of communal living when her mobility diminished and her health became more fragile.

Robert proposed that, since Gwen had decided to move into care, that he would collaborate with her to see if there were suitable facilities in Canberra. He and Peter were in Canberra now and Annette was living in Bowral, two hour's drive from Canberra. Robert and Nicola had moved to Canberra in November 2005 so that he could take up an academic position at the Australian National University. They were now in a townhouse on the shores of Lake Tuggeranong where Nicola had a studio to further her career as an artist. Gwen had been coming to Canberra for Christmas with Peter and Rhonda and their boys, David and Alex, for many years, so she was familiar with the environment. Gwen agreed to participate in exploring

Two friends visiting Gwen in Canberra circa 2009

Gwen at her 85th Birthday party in Tecoma in 2010 with Kaye, her cousin and long time close friend at the back, her sister Barbara (left) and daughter Helen (right)

the Canberra option and lived with Robert and Nicola for several weeks and visited a number of nursing homes.

By coincidence a new Catholic Church-owned facility had just opened in Garran. This newly-built Southern Cross Village was fully subscribed, but as luck would have it, Robert was able to negotiate for Gwen to get a ground floor brand new room with an ensuite that no one had occupied before. Gwen felt that this unforeseen fortuitous opportunity was 'the finger of God' pointing her to Canberra. She accepted residency at Southern Cross Village. Helen and Don were most helpful in assisting Gwen to pack up what she would need in Canberra and sell her furniture and other household items in her flat at Tecoma. Gwen was decluttering her life and moving from Melbourne after living there for most of her 81 years. It was a big call.

Just before her move to Canberra Robert drove Gwen to Ferntree Gully and accompanied her on one of her last trips to the shops. Everyone from the Post Office staff to the supermarket checkout girls knew her. She acknowledged and chatted with each of them, addressing them by their name and knowing something about their personal lives. Despite the pain of walking with a frame and her chronic breathlessness, she was still determined to get out and shine her light with people and share her optimistic good humour, as well as enjoy their humanity. Gwen was going to be missed at the Ferntree Gully shops and at St Thomas More's Parish.

The facilities in Canberra met everyone's approval. Though she would miss her mother terribly, Helen was happy that Gwen was in modern facilities close to three of her children and several grandchildren rather than in a distant suburb from her and Don and their boys, Steven and Tony, persevering in inferior facilities. Helen and Don visited Canberra whenever they could. One of the special days in Canberra was the annual get-together on Boxing Day at Robert and Nicola's town house at Greenway when all of Gwen's children and grandchildren gathered for a BBQ lunch. Gwen thoroughly enjoyed these occasions.

Gwen and Barbara at a family reunion in Canberra in 2008

Ill health was still challenging Gwen, and mobility and breathlessness were two increasing limitations to her quality of life. She went to the Aquatic Centre at Tuggeranong several times a week with Robert and Nicola to exercise in a warm wading pool with easy access designed for seniors. Though not one for Bingo or frequent outings, Gwen developed a number of friendships at Southern Cross, Garran, both among residents and staff. Gwen was happy in Canberra and had plenty of contact with Robert and Nicola, as well as Peter's wife Rhonda, who visited Gwen frequently.

2009 would prove to be another year of Breen family crisis. The sudden death of Tony, Helen's younger son at 23 years of age on Anzac Day from an accidental drug overdose, hit everyone very hard. For Helen and Don the sudden death of another child was devastating. Tony had been living independently for a couple of years in a flat that Helen had arranged for him. He was successfully employed as a plasterer and was a generous friend and likeable young man. Robert and Annette joined Helen and Don in Melbourne as soon as they could. There was much to do. The shock left them all struggling to finalise Tony's affairs before his funeral. Robert and Don found clearing and cleaning Tony's flat heart breaking.

The funeral in Melbourne was awash with emotion and bewilderment. Why did such a lovely young man have to take the risk that he did with drugs?

Steven, Helen and Tony Dawson circa 2006

He deserved a full life and a future of fulfilment, fatherhood and family life. This tragic misadventure of youth was to have unexpected and unhelpful repercussions for Gwen and her children as they all tried to help each other and come to terms with this loss in their own ways.

Annette and her boys had always been close with Helen and Don. She insisted that they accompany her and Alex and Phillip, her younger sons, on an overseas holiday to try and act as a circuit breaker on overwhelming grief and anguish. For Robert, Tony's death reminded him graphically of the dangers that had threatened his son, Ben, during his wayward years. He did his best to comfort Helen and Don, but was more of a counsellor than an emotionally connected brother. Helen and Don felt that he had not done enough. For his part, Peter kept his own counsel and did not engage, as was his way for coping with family crises.

For Gwen, Tony's death had a profound effect. He had been a shy boy with whom she had a special relationship. She had lost touch with him because she was in Canberra. She had been rushed to hospital on several occasions in the early hours with breathing difficulties and was now less able to travel and keep in touch with her Melbourne-based family and friends. As she had done after Cassie's death all those years before, she reached out to Helen and Don as best as she could to comfort them, but distance and her own fragile health made it difficult to be as supportive as she could when she lived in Melbourne close to them.

Life in Canberra was as happy as it could be under the circumstances. She enjoyed contact with Robert and Nicola and Rhonda, who was a loyal and caring person in Gwen's life, as well as Annette, who drove down from Bowral periodically. One affirming experience occurred later in 2009 when Professor Mick Dodson, the Australian of the Year, and guest speaker at a Podmore Foundation dinner announced that the inaugural Gwen Breen Commemorative Scholarship would be awarded to Lyric Hearn, an Indigenous girl from Cairns who was enrolled as boarder at Canberra Girls Grammar School. Robert and his daughter, Kelly, as well as their friends who knew her and were inspired by Gwen, were the main contributors to this scholarship. Most funds were raised through participation in the famous City2Surf Run in Sydney. Lyric was a fitting recipient because she came from a solo parent home and battled with mental health issues caused by childhood trauma.[35]

Several months after Tony's death, Helen reached out to Gwen and asked her to come back to Melbourne where she would nurse her in her new home at Upwey. She needed her mother and Gwen agreed to return, telling Robert that she knew Helen well and had to return to Melbourne because she feared that Tony's death might lead Helen to self-harm. Gwen and Helen ignored Robert's advice that accommodating Gwen at Helen's place, even if renovated to allow her to move about along rails and ascend the outside stairs in an electric lift, was a mistake. He feared that Gwen would be 'at risk' and Helen and Don's best efforts would fall short of Gwen's expectations.

Accommodating Gwen with Helen and Don did not work out as they had hoped. Helen found a room at a modern facility at the Regis Lake Park aged accommodation only 200 metres from St Thomas the Apostle Church, Blackburn. Gwen found solace, comfort and inspiration there from attending the Masses delivered by Missionaries of the Sacred Heart priests, Father Chris Murphy and Father Frank Dineen. By this time Gwen could only move by motorised wheelchair for longer distances and on a frame for short walks. Two men from the St Vincent de Paul Society at St Thomas's, Allan and Peter, took turns to escort her to church every Sunday for Mass—rain, hail or shine.

Life for Gwen at Regis Park was good. Helen visited frequently and Robert dropped in once a month or so as his business or following the Swans annual premiership campaign took him to Melbourne. First priority for Robert on these visits was to buy 'old style' battered fish and chips at the local Blackburn shops and bring them to Gwen for gleeful consumption— comfort food for Gwen since childhood. Several Melbourne friends could also visit Gwen which was something she had missed in Canberra. Marie Sheahan was back in her life again.

Gwen adapted to her circumstances and made the best of them. Her default button was to be positive. On one occasion when Annette made her

Gwen coming back smiling in her wheelchair from Mass on a rainy day in her pink Women's Breast Cancer poncho, with Robert in 2011

Gwen at Melissa's wedding on 16 April 2011

Annette and her three sons at Melissa's wedding

weekly telephone call Gwen told her that she was living the happiest days of her life at Regis Park. She was knitting blankets for others. She had all the care she needed for her medical conditions. She had a shower every morning. Food was fine. TV was interesting and she had visitors. She could call out on the phone anytime, chat, read books, say her prayers and attend Mass each Sunday, as well as on important feast days. She finished her chat with Annette giving her signature farewell, 'Love you, over and out'. After the traumas of nursing Gwen in her home, Helen had done a great job in settling her into Regis Park so she could spend her final couple of years happily. Gwen's days were spent praying, watching what she called 'My soapies', and keeping up with correspondence to her many friends in Australia and those friends she had made on her overseas trips.

In April 2011 Melissa, Gwen's special granddaughter, married Justin Stock, whom she had met at Uluru several years before. This was a great gathering of family and friends in the Hills. Helen and Don were very proud parents and Melissa was marrying into a large loving family. Gwen was well enough to attend and enjoyed the day immensely. She was very proud of the young woman that Melissa had become and delighted that she had met Justin a kind and considerate soul mate.

The New Year of 2012 was a difficult time for Gwen. A number of ailments were worsening. She could no longer get in and out of bed. She felt humiliated that staff had to lift her in a sling to take her to and from the toilet and shower each day. They had to do everything for her. Her heart was giving out. Her breathlessness was permanent and occasionally distressing as her heart struggled to pump blood and her lungs tried desperately to draw oxygen from the restricted blood flow around her body. There was fluid on her lungs that put further pressure on her cardio-vascular system. On top of these conditions was a recurring back pain that kept her in bed for long periods, lying flat out on her back looking at the ceiling.

Her 87th birthday was approaching on 11 January 2012. The weekend before her birthday her sister, Barbara, and nephew, Bernard, visited her

Gwen sitting, Sally (Steven's future wife) Don, Helen, Melissa, Justin Stock (groom) and Steven

Barbara O'Meara (Melican) at Melissa's wedding

Emma Milde (David's future wife) David, Peter and Rhonda,
with second son Alexander Breen

Robert and Nicola at Melissa's wedding 2011

on Saturday and brought her favourite meal of fish and chips and dim sims in soy sauce. This was a lovely gesture and kindness as they had to travel from Ballarat and Geelong respectively to be with Gwen. Many happy reminiscences were shared.

On Wednesday 11 January 2012 Gwen turned 87 and was a bit teary because she was in pain from a rash as well as her back. Robert had spoken to her in the morning and tried to comfort her. He rang again later in the day to see how she was going. Three things had occurred that had lifted her spirits. The first was a surprise visit from five dear friends whom she always referred to when speaking to others as 'her deserted wives'. Among what might be described as her guardian angels was Marie Sheahan, Mum's devoted and loving friend of many years. These generous and marvellous ladies cheered her up on her birthday.

The second event was the arrival of about 20 staff and residents at Regis Park in her room to acknowledge her and sing 'Happy Birthday'. Gwen told Robert that it was a crush of people in a traffic jam of wheelers. This informal Regis Park Tabernacle Choir lifted Gwen when she needed it.

Gwen in healthier times with her sister, Barbara, and her favourite nephew and Barbara's oldest son, Bernard. Barbara and Bernard visited Gwen for her 87th Birthday in 2012, a week before Gwen passed.

The third event was the arrival of a bunch of red roses from her daughters, Helen and Annette and their children, who were on holidays in Thailand. There had also been several phone calls from other family members and friends. For many of these callers, this would be the last time they spoke with Gwen. They would have been comforted to know that they lifted Gwen's spirits when she needed it. It was fair repayment. Gwen had done so much in her life to lift the spirits of others during their trials and it was lovely to know that she was supported in the same way when she was at a low ebb.

On the Saturday after her birthday, Robert and his wife, Nicola, travelled down from Canberra and Kelly and her fiancé, Clint, travelled down from Sydney. They found Gwen lying on her back and in pain. They did their best to lift her spirits with fish and chips and dim sims in soy sauce but Gwen was uncharacteristically not hungry. She assured everyone that she would rally and that her back pain would be treated. She hoped that she would be able to sit up in due course to watch her soapies. For Robert this was a distressing visit because he felt that she was in her final days or, at best, had a week or so to live. However, Gwen had rallied remarkably after shoulder surgery some months before and could do so again. Robert had made a personal vow that he would not allow his mother to die alone in care. He was torn about whether he should stay and maintain a vigil until Gwen improved or trust that she was right and once again would rally. Deeply saddened by Gwen's condition, Robert, Nicola, Kelly and Clint returned home.

On Monday evening 16 January, Melissa, the much-loved granddaughter with whom Gwen maintained a very special relationship, rang and they chatted. Gwen told Melissa of the onset of back pain and the situation with other ailments, but did not dwell on any of these conditions. She was never one for self-pity or burdening others with long conversations about her deteriorating circumstances. She ended the phone call with another of her typical optimistic saying with love. 'Melissa I don't want you to worry, Angel. It's all under control.' Gwen never left a caller or a visitor feeling worse for having spoken with her, or to feel sorry for her in any way.

Gwen died in the early hours of 17 January from congestive heart failure a few hours after speaking with Melissa.[36] Robert would say at her funeral:

> It is comforting to know that Mum died in her sleep on Tuesday and that her time to leave us was the right time. It is comforting to know that she felt that she had done all that she could for her children, and her family and friends. She was leading a very dependent life, accompanied by pain that did not suit her. She would want us to be happy that she has now achieved a blessed release.

A member of staff notified Robert in Canberra at around 7am under arrangements he had made with the staff there during an earlier visit. Helen and Annette were returning from their holiday at the time and were due to land in Sydney later that day. Helen had left instructions at Regis Lake Park that a relative in Melbourne was to be notified if there was an emergency affecting Gwen. Robert spoke with that relative suggesting that it would be better to wait until Helen and Annette were clear of customs and each had arrived home before passing on the news of Gwen's death. His advice was not accepted. Helen and Annette received the news by text when they turned on their mobile phones after landing.

The next 72 hours were busy ones organising Gwen's funeral for Friday 20 January and notifying family and friends. Gwen's funeral was held at St Thomas the Apostle, Blackburn. She had already made arrangements with Robert on the order of service, readings and hymns. He had booklets printed and sent to Melbourne before coming down to finalise arrangements with Helen, who did a great job contacting everyone who would have wanted to pay their last respects.

In his eulogy, Robert characterised the funeral as a farewell, stating:

> We are not farewelling a great Australian today who achieved fame, fortune or public attention. We are saying farewell to a magnificent mother who stood by her four kids while suffering many adversities. We are saying farewell to a caring grandmother who did her best in the years of physical decline.

We are saying farewell to a mighty, mighty woman who gave counsel and optimistic uplifting friendship to casualties of marital breakdown and mental illness so they could follow her example, persevere and carry on.

We are saying farewell to a great humanitarian who helped others in many different ways.

Above all, we are saying good bye to someone who has run the good race, kept the faith, loved her God with all of her heart, and touched many lives along the way.

After Robert's eulogy, he invited anyone who wished to say something about Gwen to come forward. Two women did so. One, who remembered Gwen from the retreats she organised for the Supporting Mother's Association, spoke movingly about the impact of Gwen's out-reach to her and others The other woman spoke of Gwen's kindness to those who were suffering from the trauma of childhood sexual abuse. Finally, Allen, one of the men from the St Vincent de Paul Society, went to the microphone and spoke of Gwen's contribution St Thomas the Apostle Parish during the time she had been in care at Regis Park. These were fitting tributes to Gwen who never lost the gift of caring and affirming communications with others, even when her own circumstances were not the best. Measured in the lives she touched and her own honourable and virtuous conduct, Gwen Breen could rightfully be dubbed as a 'great Australian'.

Gwen was cremated at the Springvale Botanical Cemetery. Robert accompanied her coffin to the crematorium with his daughter, Kelly, and her fiancé, Clint, following an Army tradition of ensuring a comrade arrives safely at their final resting place. Helen is the custodian of Gwen's ashes. Gwen bequeathed her estate to her four children 'as tenants in common in equal shares absolutely for their own use and benefit.'

Endnotes

1. Thank you to my Aunt Barbara, Gwen's younger sister, for researching and finding the information for this section on the Irish and British immigrant origins of the Melbourne-based O'Meara-Allsop clan. For reasons that become obvious later in the narrative, I have offered neither information on nor have any interest in discovering the origins of my father's family. The challenge for whomever inherits the 'historian gene' among the coming generations is to research and tell the story of Gwen's Irish-British ancestors.

2. Named after his father, but nicknamed from his second name, John, and called Jack,

3. Letter, Brian O'Meara, circa 1995.

4. On the day of his funeral one newspaper opined: 'Taylor was a criminal of ordinary mentality, whose distinguishing features were his callous disregard for the lives of others, his treachery towards his associates, and his personal cowardice.' http://trove.nla.gov.au/newspaper/article/24206534 accessed 14 April 2016.

5. Thank you to Martin Melican, who gleaned and shared this information about Uncle Charlie from the Melbourne newspapers of the time containing references to court proceedings and events related to both Squizzy Taylor and Charlie Allsop.

6. See Russell Robinson and Jo Lyons (ed.), *Khaki Crims and Desperadoes*, Pan Macmillan, Melbourne 2014 for more on Charlie and Robert Allsop.

7. http://www.spbookmaker.com.au/ accessed 13 April 2016.

8. Gwen Breen, typed notes circa 1995.

9. Ibid. Certificate of Baptism, Barbara Frances O'Meara, 23 June 1999 signed by Monsignor G. Cudmore. Barbara's godparents were Andrew O'Meara and May Manly.

10. Letter, Brian O'Meara, circa 1995.

11. Certificate of Baptism, 19 September 1985 signed by Fr G. Maher, Parish Priest. Anne's godparents were Michael and Susan Gallagher

12. Certificate of Baptism, 19 September 1985 signed by Fr G. Maher, Parish Priest. Brian's godparent was Alexa Nangavione.

13. Certificate of Baptism, 19 September 1985 signed by Fr G. Maher, Parish Priest. Peter's godparents were William and Frances Birks.

14. Gwen Breen, handwritten essay, circa 1996.

15. Ibid.

16. Most houses had ice boxes rather than electric refrigerators. Food was kept cold by keeping blocks of ice in an upper compartment of the ice box. Mr Pimm was one of the many 'ice men' who bought blocks of ice from the factory to households at a sale price of six pence a block.

17. Gwen Breen, written essay, circa 1996.

18. Paul McGuire and Frances Margaret McGuire, *The Price of Admiralty*, Oxford University Press: Melbourne, 1944, p. 125 and 128.

19. Ibid, p. 192.

20. Ibid, p. 263.

21. Ibid, p. 264.

22. Ibid, p. 268.

23. Ibid, p. 307.

24. Gwen Breen, letter of 24 August 1995, p. 2.

25. Royal Park Psychiatric Hospital Examination File- Gweneth Patricia Breen, 22 November 1962.

26. Royal Park Psychiatric Hospital Examination File- Gweneth Patricia Breen, 13 December 1962.

27. Royal Park Psychiatric Hospital Examination File- Gweneth Patricia Breen, 25 January 1963.

28. Gwen used the term 'twerp' to describe a man who was unreasonable, petty and selfish.

29. Royal Park Psychiatric Hospital Examination File- Gweneth Patricia Breen, 25 January 1963.

30. Letter, Jan Pink, 1995.

31. Letter, Mary Spittall, 1995.

32. Letter, J.E. Brown, Staff Officer Records for Director of Sailor's Postings to Mrs J. (sic) Melican, N85/2523 DSP/ 1587/85, 20 June 1985.

33. After a period of public consultation, in July 1995 the Aboriginal flag was proclaimed a 'Flag of Australia' under the Flags Act 1953.

34. John Cooke, 'Abused? Then share the pain', Whitehorse Post, 29 July 1998, p. 2.

35. In 2007 Robert had joined several Duntroon classmates to incorporate the Podmore Foundation with the motto Returning Opportunity as a not-for-profit organisation in the ACT. The founders were either sons from immigrant or solo parent families. They founded Podmore in gratitude for the great education that had received at Duntroon and wanted to give young people from disadvantaged backgrounds access to a good education in good company. Lyric would go on to complete her secondary schooling at Canberra Girls Grammar School in 2016.

36. Death Certificate 22143/2012, 1 February 2012.

www.ingramcontent.com/pod-product-compliance
Lightning Source LLC
Chambersburg PA
CBHW060052100426
42742CB00014B/2786